Configuring US Benefits with SAP

Satish Badgi

Contents

Preface		3
Purpose of this Book		3
Structure of the Book		3
Acknowledgments		3

1 Benefits Processes ... 5
- 1.1 Understanding the Employee Life Cycle ... 6
- 1.2 New Hire Enrollment ... 7
- 1.3 Changes to Benefits ... 8
- 1.4 Terminations ... 9
- 1.5 COBRA Processing ... 9
  - Entitlement for COBRA ... 9
  - Qualified COBRA Events ... 10
  - Qualified Beneficiaries ... 10
  - Process ... 10
- 1.6 Flexible Spending Account and Claims Process ... 10
- 1.7 Summary ... 10

2 Baseline Configuration for Benefits Administration ... 13
- 2.1 Prerequisites ... 13
- 2.2 Benefits Areas and Basic Settings ... 13
  - Benefits Area ... 14
  - Benefit Providers ... 15
  - Plan Types ... 16
  - Plan Status ... 16
- 2.3 First and Second Program Grouping ... 16
  - First Program Grouping ... 16
  - Second Program Grouping ... 17
  - Define Benefit Programs ... 18
- 2.4 Managing Eligibility ... 18
  - Eligibility Groupings ... 18
  - Eligibility Variants ... 19
  - Eligibility Rules ... 19
  - Dynamic Eligibility ... 20
- 2.5 Managing Dependent Eligibility ... 20
  - Dependent Eligibility Variant ... 20
  - Dependent Eligibility Rule ... 20
- 2.6 Termination ... 21
  - Termination Groupings ... 21
  - Termination Variant ... 22
  - Termination Rules ... 22
- 2.7 Adjustment Reasons ... 22
  - Adjustment Reason Groupings ... 22
  - Adjustment Reasons ... 23
  - Linking Plan with Grouping and Reasons ... 23
- 2.8 How It Works ... 24
- 2.9 Summary ... 25

3 Plan Configuration ... 27
- 3.1 Defining Employee Groupings ... 27
  - Define Employee Criteria Groups ... 27
  - Define Cost Groupings ... 28
  - Defining Coverage Groupings ... 29
  - Employee Contribution Grouping ... 29
  - Define Employer Contribution Grouping ... 30
- 3.2 Health Plans ... 30
  - Plan General Data ... 30
  - Options for Health Plans ... 30
  - Dependent Coverage Options ... 31
  - Defining Cost Variants and Rules ... 31
  - Managing Plan Attributes ... 32
  - Testing the Configuration ... 32
- 3.3 Insurance Plans ... 32
  - Plan General Data ... 33
  - Define Coverage Variants and Rules ... 33
  - Define Cost Variants and Rules ... 34

Contents

	Managing Plan Attributes	34
	What is an Imputed Income?	34
3.4	Savings Plans	35
	Plan General Data	35
	Employee Contribution Variants and Rules	35
	Manage Plan Atrributes	37
	Define Vesting Rule	37
	Managing Investments for Savings Plans	37
	Testing the Configuration	38
3.5	Flexible Spending Account (FSA) Plans	38
	Plan General Data	38
	Spending Account Attributes	38
	Defining Claim Types	39
	Testing the Configuration	39
3.6	Miscellaneous Plans	40
	Plan General Data	40
	Defining Cost Variants and Rules	40
	Manage Plan Attributes	41
	Testing the Configuration	41
3.7	COBRA	41
	Defining Relevance for COBRA	42
	Qualifying Events Management	42
	Assign COBRA Events to Personnel Actions	42
	Define Processing Parameters for Benefits Area	42
3.8	Summary	42

4	**Managing Benefits Administration**	45
4.1	Enrollment Monitor	45
	New Hire Elections/Enrollment	46

	Employee Life Event Changes	48
	Open Enrollment Elections	49
4.2	Termination Monitor	49
4.3	Managing COBRA	50
4.4	Useful Tools	51
	Overview of Plans	51
	Plan Cost Summary	51
	Configuration Consistency Check	52
	Overview of Adjustment Permissions	52
4.5	Summary	53

5	**Technical Support**	55
5.1	Forms	55
5.2	User Exits	56
5.3	Interfaces	57
5.4	Data Conversion	58
5.5	Basics of Employee Self Service (ESS)	58
5.6	SAP Benefits in an Outsourced Payroll Environment	60
5.7	Benefits Schemas	60
5.8	Summary	61

A	**Life Plan Configuration Sheet**	63
B	**Model Wage Types for Benefits**	65
C	**Typical Benefits Terminology Questions**	69
	Index	73

Preface

SAP's Benefits module has a matured functionality which was developed over many versions. When it comes to addressing the US Benefits, SAP Benefits module coupled with Employee Self Service (ESS) is a strong combination. However, sometimes the Benefits User's community is commonly divided over the debate of insourcing versus outsourcing. There are many organizations that outsource their benefits because they do not want to manage the benefit administration. While there are others who believe it is a good idea to keep it in-house, there are many SAP customers who prefer in-house Benefits implementations. SAP's benefits configuration drives the automation and ease of use for the end users. SAP has provided a lot of flexibility around the configuration, and understanding of the features, groupings, cost variants, and many such functionalities in the module are crucial to the success of your implementation. If you follow a logical path to the configuration, it is not as difficult or complex as some other areas in SAP — such as Time Evaluation or Payroll Rules!

This book starts with the Benefits processes that you need to know in order to configure them effectively. These processes are discussed around the employee work and life events that drive Benefits. Subsequently, the book dives into the base configuration for groupings, benefit areas, and other eligibility related variants. I have attempted to structure this book with a logical flow of a configuration. In the absence of this flow, I find that the configurators can easily get confused with different groupings and features.

Purpose of this Book

This book is written to assist readers with the configuration of their SAP US Benefits through the use of many practical examples. It is expected that readers are well familiar with the Personnel Administration (PA) module and the concept of "Features."

Structure of the Book

The book is divided into five main chapters. It starts with an overview of the benefits processes in the first chapter, followed by details about the base configuration in chapter two. Chapter three addresses the configuration related to different types of benefit plans, and chapter four is more oriented toward the application or usage of the benefits module. In this chapter we will relate the configuration to benefits administration. Chapter five discusses some of the essential technical topics, including Interfaces and User Exits, which are inevitable in any US Benefits implementation.

Acknowledgments

This second book is for the second generation in my family — Shivani, Aarati, Chintamani, Rasika, Shubhankar, Amol, and Anushree. I guess the excitement of my first book was so much among my family and friends that I had no choice but to gather my thoughts together to complete this second book. The positive feedback from my readers for the first book on US Payroll also gave me tremendous encouragement to complete this second book. My sincere thanks to my editor Jenifer Niles for her patience and support during the entire publishing process.

Please continue to write to me at *saphrwriter@yahoo.com* with your feedback, comments and inputs.

1 Benefits Processes

Before discussing the benefits of configuration, it is important to review the benefits processes as they occur in a typical organization. Without understanding the processes, you run the risk of getting lost in the technical details of the different benefits groupings and their associated features. If you understand the processes well, you will be able to run the configuration effectively.

Using the classic employee life-cycle approach always makes things clearer in the SAP HR world. Therefore, we will start our discussion with a review of the classic life-cycle model, which includes hiring, promotions, different work and life events, and termination. From there, we will learn about the benefits module as it relates to the life cycle.

Please keep in mind that any discussion of benefits, by necessity, must be very country specific, so this book is focused primarily on US benefits. The topics will generally be applicable across SAP versions 4.7, ECC 5.0, and ECC 6.0. In most US companies, the benefits package for employees covers many of the following:

- Health plans
- Life insurance plans
- 401k plans
- Other retirement savings plans (403B, 457) and pension plans
- Stock options
- Various leave and vacation plans, including parental leave
- Tuition reimbursement
- Flexible work schedules

However, in the world of SAP HCM Payroll and Benefits, these get divided between different sub-modules.

Example

Flexible work schedules can fall under Time Management, while tuition reimbursement can be just a wage type in Payroll.

For the purpose of our discussion in this book, we will focus on the benefit plans that fall within SAP's benefit modules.

These include:
- Health plans
  - Health
  - Dental
  - Vision
- Life plans
  - Basic life
  - AD&D
  - Dependent life
- Savings plans
  - 401k plans — with employer match
  - 403B plans — with employer match
  - Catch up contributions
- Deferred income and pension plans
- Stock plans
- Flexible spending accounts
  - Health care
  - Dependent care
- Miscellaneous plans — Examples:
  - Health club membership
  - Pet insurance
  - Company car
- Vacation and holiday plans

> **Note**
> SAP uses the Miscellaneous plan functionality for other benefit plans that do not fit into the normal plan categories, such as pet insurance and gym membership.

1.1 Understanding the Employee Life Cycle

Figure 1.1 presents a view of benefits administration as triggered by different employee events and the resulting post-benefits processes. The events are categorized as Life- and Work-related events as shown in the columns in the figure. The employee work events start with a New Hire event and then pass through many additional events, such as Promotions, Transfers, and in some cases Terminations or employee separations. Employee life events include things like marriage, divorce, childbirth/adoption, and similar events. The employee life cycle starts with hiring and can have a logical end point with termination or retirement. The concept of work and life events therefore has an impact on the benefits. These events serve as a central theme to the benefits administration.

So what does SAP Benefits have to do with work and life events? Well, pretty much everything. The U.S. Department of Labor (*www.dol.gov*) administers benefits laws through the Employee Benefits Security Administration (EBSA). Marriage, divorce, birth or adoption, and death are the life events that may necessitate a change in your benefits coverage. In addition, the Health Insurance Portability and Accountability Act (HIPAA) requires that a special enrollment period be made available for certain life events. The Benefits module configuration therefore goes hand in hand with these regulations. As much as we need to learn the configuration, we also need to be familiar with these regulations.

> **Example**
> You have to allow 30 days after childbirth for the employee to add a child as a new dependent.

As you start configuring the system, you will notice that these events and the associated eligibility of employees for specific plans are closely linked. In addition, SAP's Personnel Administration (PA) module with its associated HR structures has a large impact on the Benefits module configuration. The Benefits module probably has the largest number of technical features of any SAP HR module (they can be accessed through Transaction PE03). All of these features drive decisions using HR structural elements: personnel area, sub-area, employee group, sub-group, organizational unit, etc.

You may also have to do Consolidated Omnibus Reconciliation Act (COBRA) processing as the result of work and life events. We will learn more about COBRA later in this chapter.

The events result in different benefits-related processing as shown on the right hand side of Figure 1.1.

These include:

- Enrolling in the benefits plan
- Changing plans
- Terminating benefits
- Offering COBRA benefits upon termination
- Sending data to the benefit providers

During the employee life cycle and the associated events, four entities are involved in the process:

- Employee
- Employer
- Benefit Provider
- Service Provider (doctors)

Of these four, we will only focus on the first three for the purposes of this book. Figure 1.2 shows a very high-level information exchange between these entities, and Table 1.1 explains Figure 1.2 further.

Transfer Between Entities	Type of Information Exchange
Employee and Employer	▸ Plan selections ▸ Plan changes ▸ Dependent details ▸ Eligibility
Employer and Benefits Providers	▸ Enrollment and changes ▸ Employee and the dependent data
Benefit providers and Employee	▸ Web-based access to plan data and information

Table 1.1 Data Transfer in Benefits Processing

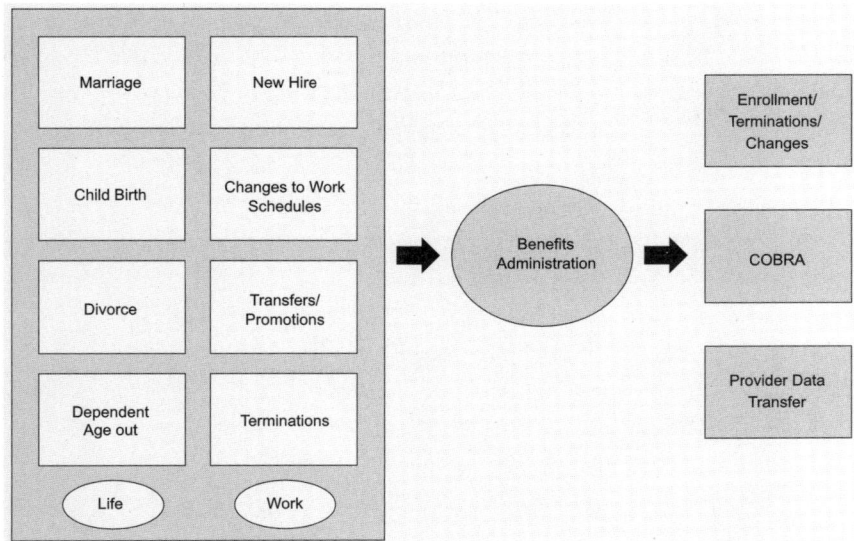

Figure 1.1 Benefits Administration View

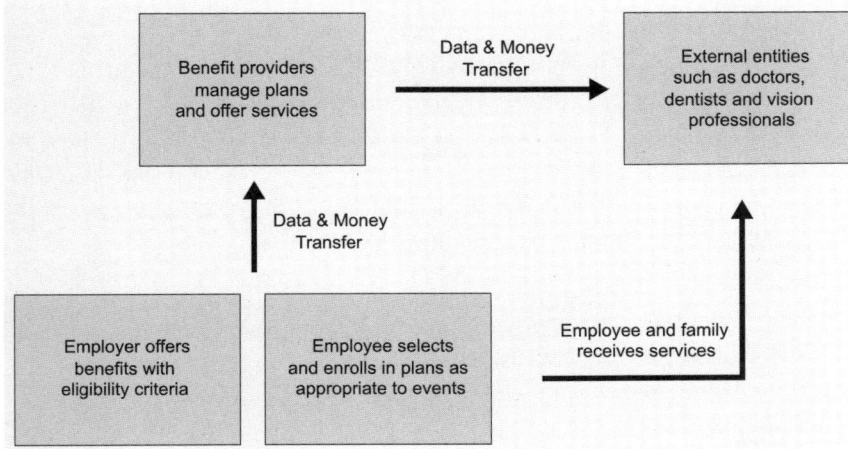

Figure 1.2 Benefits Data Flow

In Chapter 3, we will discuss the configuration of different types of plans. You will see that in any typical organization you have to address multiple interfaces for the different data and information-transfer situations.

For now, we will start the process discussion with the New Hire and Enrollment Process.

1.2 New Hire Enrollment

The benefits process starts with enrollment of newly hired employees. New employees will have been sent, or will receive on their first day, a benefits information kit explaining the plans, eligibility, and rules related to the benefits.

> **Example**
> Some organizations enroll new employees on the first of every month; therefore, employees who join in the middle of month have a waiting period before their benefits coverage starts. In addition, depending upon the level of employee as well as the organization's policies, the employee is eligible for certain benefit plans. For example, senior-level people may have health-club membership benefits.

The enrollment in benefits plans can occur twice, once when an employee joins the organization and then again during annual enrollment. In the U.S., each organization has an annual open-enrollment period when employees can choose from different plan options. Typically, companies start the new plans in January, so the open enrollment period usually occurs during the months of November and December of the prior year. These enrollments can be processed as follows:

- Using SAP Employee Self Service (ESS) where employees do self enrollment.
- Using Third Party Benefits Service Providers. Some companies contract with providers like Hewitt to manage the enrollment. Employees use the portal from these third party providers to enroll. In situations like these, an interface will be required between the external system and SAP Benefits.
- Having the benefits administrator carry out the enrollment based on paper forms.
- Using a telephone-based system.

The SAP back-end configuration and table maintenance remains the same, regardless of the mode of enrollment. During the enrollment, the employee will have to select from the plans for which they are eligible. You may be familiar with the Personnel Actions in the PA module in SAP. Personnel actions are accessed through the PA40 Transaction in PA. With respect to hiring an employee, in Chapter 2, we will discuss the use of infotype 0378 for linking the PA and Benefits module. The actual new-hire enrollment process will differ across organizations. Figure 1.3 presents the high-level enrollment process to show that — based on eligibility criteria and organizational policies — employees can enroll in different plans. The result of enrollment in SAP involves the creation of infotypes and the generation of confirmation letters. It is not our intention to discuss the Benefits infotypes, because plenty of information is available in SAP's standard documentation (http://help.sap.com). However, let us quickly list them as a reference because they will be used in the discussion throughout the rest of book. Benefits infotypes:

- 0167 Health Plans
- 0168 Insurance Plans
- 0169 Savings Plans
- 0170 Flexible Spending Plans
- 0378 Adjustment Reasons
- 0377 Miscellaneous Plans
- 0171 General Benefits (Benefits Program Groupings)

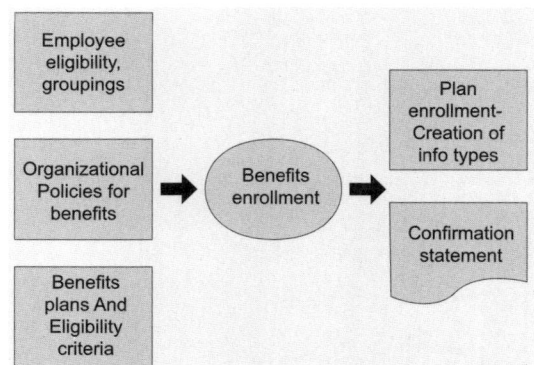

Figure 1.3 High-Level View of Enrollment Process

1.3 Changes to Benefits

From Figure 1.1 earlier, it was clear that any of the work and life events can potentially change the benefits. Table 1.2 shows the sample situations around changes to benefits based on life or work events.

Description of Event	Possible Impact on Benefits
Life Events	
When an employee becomes a parent by birth or by adoption	Enroll the child in benefit plans such as health and dental
Marriage	Enroll the spouse in qualified plans. Add a beneficiary.
Divorce	Changes to benefits as well as COBRA events
A dependent has come of age and moved out of house	Terminate benefits for dependent
Unfortunate event of employee death	COBRA event for beneficiaries
Work Events	
New hire	Enrollment in qualified plans (A qualified plan is established by employers to extend retirement benefits to employees and their beneficiaries)

Table 1.2 Impact of Life Events on Benefits

Description of Event	Possible Impact on Benefits
Termination or separation	Termination of benefits
Leave of absence	Changes to benefits as per policies

Table 1.2 Impact of Life Events on Benefits (cont.)

You will notice that most of these life events will translate to a transaction in SAP for maintaining employee master data. Therefore the Benefits module needs to work with the employee master data appropriately. We will discuss the linkage and the dependent configuration in Chapter 2. Infotype 0378 plays a major role in this linkage between PA and the Benefits module. These and similar other qualified events also have a standard period (typically 30 calendar days) within which the employee needs to contact the human resources (HR) department for appropriate changes. For our purposes, we will assume that the employee has enrolled in the benefit plans and the plans are changing as the result of these events. Figure 1.4 presents the high-level flow diagram for changes in the benefits process.

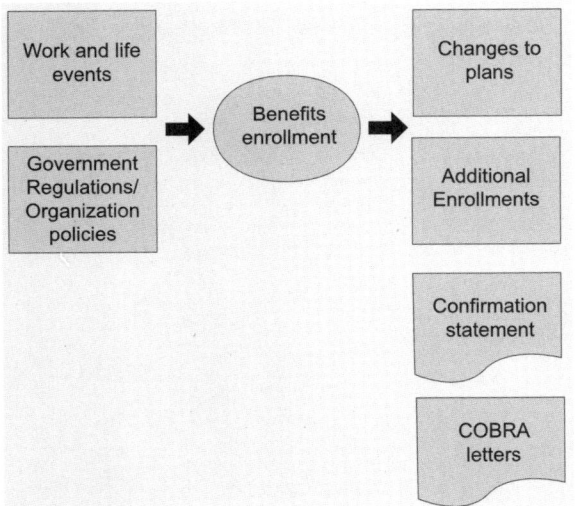

Figure 1.4 High-Level View: Changes to Benefits Process

There could be certain events that will demand enrollment of dependents, but in other cases there could be changes or terminations of plans. In each case, a document such as a conformation statement or a COBRA letter will be generated. Let us learn how the termination process affects benefits.

1.4 Terminations

When an employee separates from an organization, the benefits need to be terminated. Depending upon the organization's policies, the benefits can be terminated immediately or by the end of the calendar month. However, the other important part of the termination process is COBRA processing. According to the definition from the Department of Labor's website, COBRA gives workers and their families who lose their health benefits the choice of continuing group health benefits provided by their group health plan for limited periods of time under certain circumstances, such as voluntary or involuntary job loss, reduction in the hours worked, transition between jobs, death, divorce, and other life events. Qualified individuals may be required to pay the entire premium for coverage up to 102% of the cost to the plan.

Appropriate COBRA processing needs to be handled based on termination events in SAP. The termination process can be divided into two areas: termination of existing benefit plans in the employee's data, and generation of an appropriate letter for COBRA processing.

1.5 COBRA Processing

Figure 1.5 presents a very simple view of COBRA processing, which we will explain in this section.

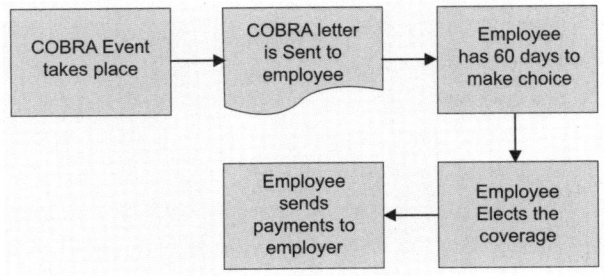

Figure 1.5 COBRA Processing

Entitlement for COBRA

Employers who offer group health plans and have more than 20 employees during at least 50% of the business days in the previous year need to offer COBRA benefits.

Qualified COBRA Events

These events are the ones that will cause the loss of health benefits for the employee or their beneficiaries. Depending upon the event, the coverage for an employee as well as their beneficiaries is decided. Here, we will give examples of qualifying events.

- **For an Employee**
  - Voluntary or involuntary termination other than for gross misconduct
  - Reduction in work hours
- **For Spouses**
  - Voluntary or involuntary termination of the covered employee other than for gross misconduct
  - Reduction in work hours for the covered employee
  - Divorce
  - Death of the covered employee
- **For Dependent Children**
  - Voluntary or involuntary termination of the covered employee other than for gross misconduct reasons
  - Reduction in work hours for the covered employee
  - Loss of dependent child status
  - Divorce
  - Death of the covered employee

Qualified Beneficiaries

Typically, a qualified beneficiary is the individual who is a spouse or dependent. The spouse or dependent needs to be in that status at least a day before the qualifying COBRA event takes place.

Process

The simple steps of the COBRA process include:

- Employers inform the plan providers within 30 days of the qualifying events.
- Employees and beneficiaries must be notified within 14 days after the plan provider receives the notice of qualifying event.
- The individual then is given 60 days to elect coverage in case he wants the COBRA continuation coverage.
- Generally COBRA covers 18 months in events such as termination and reduction in work hours and starts on the day that the coverage was lost due to a qualifying event.
- The employee/beneficiary pays for the coverage, with payment not to exceed 102 % (employee and employer costs and a 2 % administrative cost allowed).
- That covers the COBRA process. Now let's take a quick look at Flexible Spendng Accounts.

1.6 Flexible Spending Account and Claims Process

Flexible spending accounts (FSAs) are pre-tax accounts that allow the participants to set aside pre-tax money for qualified health and dependent care expenses. As a participant, you will need to submit a claim form to get the expense reimbursed from the account. FSA accounts allow employees to save on taxes for their out-of-pocket medical and dependents' care expenses. Typically, employers put a limit of $2,000–$3,000 on health care FSA accounts. There are two types of FSA: Health Care and Dependent Care. We will learn more about these in Chapter 3. There are also many resources on the Web that will give you additional information on FSAs. Figure 1.6 shows a simple representation of the process flow for FSA accounts.

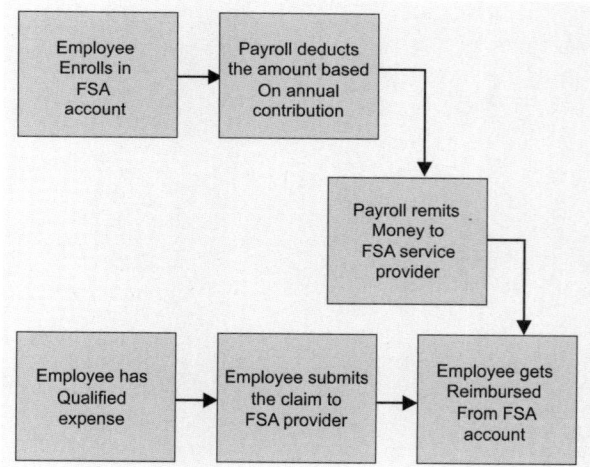

Figure 1.6 FSA Process Flow

1.7 Summary

In this chapter, we learned about the major benefits processes related to an employee's work and life events. Understanding these benefits processes will help you better understand the discussions of benefit plans, eligibility, and configuration in the next chapters. The processes have a big impact on the configuration and how you manage it using SAP's functionality. In Chapter 2, we will discuss the base configuration required for the Benefits module.

2 Baseline Configuration for Benefits Administration

Before we learn about the configuration of benefits plans, we need to learn about the baseline configuration. SAP's Benefits module uses many new concepts, such as benefits area, program groupings, and various employee groupings. In this chapter, we will learn about this prerequisite or baseline configuration.

The first step in benefits administration and managing benefits plans for employees is completing the baseline configuration or preparatory configuration. "Baseline configuration" is not a technical term, but we define it as all configuration in the SAP Benefits module that is needed before we configure benefit plans. Baseline configuration starts with benefits areas and encompasses individual employee-level configurations such as benefits grouping. This configuration gives the project team flexibility in how they handle the different rules and variations among the employee population.

To help you understand the baseline configuration, we will use a "top-down" approach, beginning with the benefits area, which is the top node, and then moving down to the employee-level groupings. At appropriate places in the chapter, we will identify the areas that are dependent on an actual plan configuration. Please note that this baseline configuration cannot be done in isolation, and you will often have to configure the plans and then repeat the baseline configuration process.

Note

Because this book is focused on benefits administration, we will not be going into depth on the conceptual details of benefits enrollment, or the rules and policies.

If you need additional information on the concepts, you can refer to standard SAP documentation (*http://help.sap.com*), or any other Web resources on benefits topics to find this information.

2.1 Prerequisites

Let us begin with a list of the prerequisites you will need to complete the configuration. Keep the items from the following list handy when you embark on the configuration activities:

- Personnel actions and Reason codes from the Personnel Administration (PA) module
- A spreadsheet showing the proposed benefit plans with eligibility definitions
- Benefits manual for your organization that explains the rules and policies to the employees
- Final HR structures (with an option to change them as per your benefits module design)
- Project schedules with clear alignment with enrollment period
- Project schedules with data conversion strategy

We start our configuration discussion with the benefits area. If you are not familiar with the features in SAP, it is a good idea to use Transaction PE03 and learn about the features before you dig deeper into the Benefits module.

2.2 Benefits Areas and Basic Settings

In this section, we will learn about configuring the benefits area along with the administrative parameters for the

2 Baseline Configuration for Benefits Administration

area. In addition, we will discuss other basic settings, including benefit plan types and benefit plan statuses.

Benefits Area

You may have heard about the payroll area in the Payroll module of SAP. The benefits area is a similar concept in the Benefits module. The benefits area allows the administrative separation of employees. This separation has to do with benefit plans rather than eligibility. You will find the typical definition factors for the benefits area listed in this sub-section. In a typical single-country implementation, you will always find a single benefits area. However, if you need to configure benefits areas from the ground up, the general rules for deciding whether it is necessary to offer one or many benefits areas are as follows:

- The benefits area involves currency, so you will definitely need an area for each currency by country.
- The benefits administration and plan management are vastly different; for example, different group companies have different benefit programs for employees.
- The benefits plan configuration is dependent on benefits area, and you will need to configure the benefits plan in each benefits area separately. We will learn in Chapter 3 how the configuration of plans is dependent on the benefits area; therefore, the more benefits areas needed, the more work you will add to the configuration.
- The benefits area also has an impact on security and authorization. The user population for benefits areas will be different from each other and hence users will be able to access the benefits area as well as plans within the benefits area as applicable for them.
- The benefits area also impacts payroll. Benefit plans have a close integration with payroll through wage types and so a direct impact on payroll configuration.

Therefore, if you're looking at a typical single country, single currency implementation, you will normally have a single benefits area. Figure 2.1 shows creation of a benefits area **SB** followed by Figure 2.2, which presents feature **BAREA**. The name **SB** has no significance and is just a two letter naming convention followed in an SAP configuration. This feature is very simple with typically one line per country logic. In this chapter, we will see more situations like those shown in Figures 2.1 and 2.2, where SAP drives the features from the configuration table using the **Feature** button. You will notice the country code in Figure 2.1, which shows that you will need at least one benefits area per country. Examples are the U.S. and Canada.

Command				
Line	Variable key	F	C	Operations
000010			D	MOLGA
000020	07			&BAREA=07,
000030	10			&BAREA=SB,

Figure 2.2 Maintaining Feature BAREA for Benefits Area

After you create the benefits area, it is essential to create administrative parameters for it. Using the IMG menu path **Benefits • Flexible Administration • Define Administrative Parameters** will lead you to this configuration. As shown in Figure 2.3 the administrative parameters control the open-enrollment dates. The example shows typical open-enrollment dates for year 2007. Normally, many employers offer a 4–6 week open-enrollment period. The open-enrollment period is the defined period in which employees are allowed to enroll in the benefit plans.

The benefits area follows the same analogy that the payroll area in the Payroll module or the Personnel area in the PA module follows. As an example, payroll-areas are separated by frequency or check dates. Personnel-area separation comes about by location or geography. Similarly, benefits-area separation is determined by differences in currency or benefit programs. In the next step, you need to establish the relationship between the employee and the benefits area. Infotype 0171 (General Benefits Information) in the employee master data establishes this. In the case of payroll, infotype 0001 links the

Benefit area	Description	Country grouping
SB	Benefits-USA	10

Figure 2.1 Creating the Benefits Area

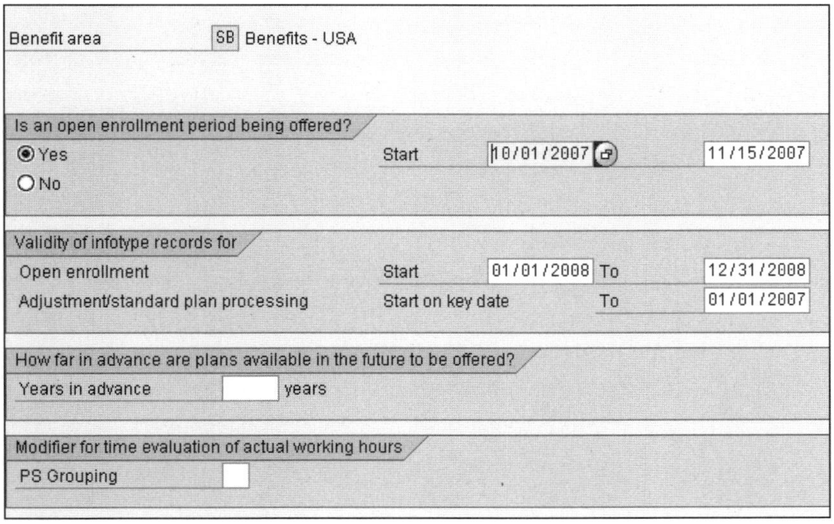

2.2 Benefits Areas and Basic Settings

Figure 2.3 Administrative Parameters for the Benefits Area

employee's payroll area; similarly, infotype 0171 links the benefits area to the employee master data. Figure 2.3 shows the Benefits Area default setting that will appear when you create this infotype. The default is based on the feature BAREA that we just configured. Now let us move on to discuss the first and second program groupings, shown in Figure 2.4. The first and second program groupings are used to drive the eligibility of plans for different types of employees. These groupings use the HR structures to drive the decisions.

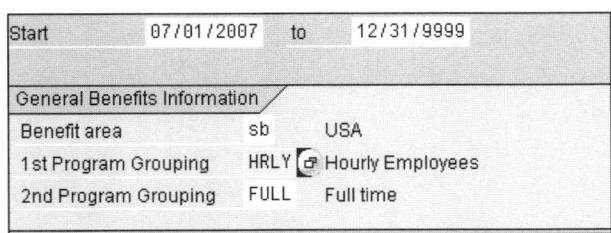

Figure 2.4 Infotype 0171 — General Benefits Information

Benefit Providers

Benefit providers are the companies that offer benefit plans. These include health-plan providers, 401k plan providers, and vision-plan providers. The IMG menu path **Benefits • Basic Settings • Define Benefit Providers** will let you create the providers you need. To create the providers, you will need a full list of providers with the data details shown in Figure 2.5. This data includes, for example, all of the health plan, insurance plan, and 401k plan providers. In larger corporations, there is more than one provider per plan type, and hence you will need to capture all of them, because both SAP Benefits and SAP Payroll modules need to send data to these benefit providers. While SAP's Benefits module sends the enrollment, employee details, and dependent details, SAP Payroll uses the third-party remittance functionality to send the deduction amounts. This payroll functionality ties together the HR payee and vendor details for a particular benefit provider to process the payments, as seen in Figure 2.5.

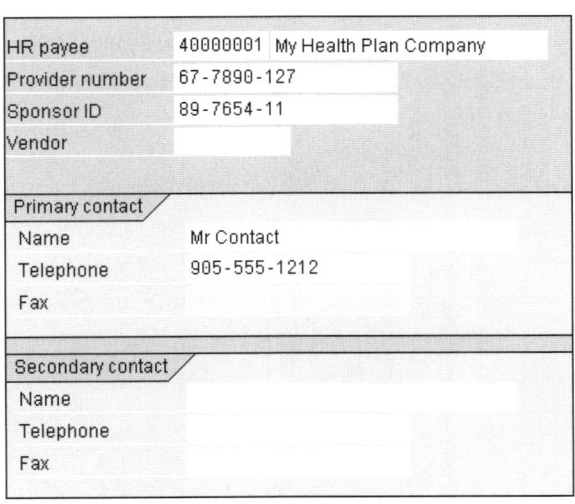

Figure 2.5 Creating a Benefit Provider

In Chapter 3, when we discuss creating plans, we will link the providers with the plans. But before we configure plan types, you need to understand that SAP has delivered plan categories. Within these plan categories, you will be able to create plan types.

Plan Types

Plan types are linked with plan categories, which include:

- A — Health plans
- B — Insurance plans
- C — Savings plans
- D — FSA plans
- E — Miscellaneous plans
- F — Stock purchase plans

You cannot create new plan categories, but you can create new plan types and link them to one of the categories as shown in Figure 2.6. If you have plans that cannot be categorized clearly, you can always use the Miscellaneous category as shown in the example in Figure 2.6. The IMG menu path **Benefits • Basic Settings • Plan Attributes • Define Benefit Plan Types** will lead you to the configuration.

Plan type	Text	Plan category	Text
401K	Savings	C	Savings plan
HLTH	Health	A	Health plan
DNTL	Dental	A	Health plan
LIFE	Insurance	B	Insurance plan
CLUB	Club	E	Miscellaneous plan

Figure 2.6 Plan Types Creation

In Chapter 3, we will link the actual plans with these plan types. The relationship linkage is **Plan categories • Plan Types • Plans** (for example, **Category-Savings Plans • Type-401k • Plan-Fidelity 401k**).

Plan Status

On an annual basis, companies have to renegotiate their plans, or negotiate with new benefit providers. In addition, companies might acquire other companies and then have to deal with merging the two companies' plans into one. In all such situations, it becomes important to manage the status of the plans. For example you will have to discontinue enrollment in the plans that are no longer applicable. The different statuses are as follows:

- **Active**
  Plans are active and employees need to enroll in them.
- **Locked**
  You have some employees enrolled in plans, but any new enrollment is not allowed.
- **Closed**
  No active employees or no new enrollment, but the plans are kept for a historical data perspective.

To configure the statuses for a benefit plan, follow the IMG menu path **Benefits • Basic Settings • Plan Attributes • Define Benefit Plan** as shown in Figure 2.7. Please note that the statuses are configured for a particular benefits area. As you perform this configuration step, the system will ask you to set a benefits area, and the statuses will then be valid for the particular benefits area. In our example, they are valid for benefits area **SB**.

PlanStatus	Text	Active	Enrollment
CO	Closed	✓	✓
OE	Open	✓	✓
LC	Locked	✓	

Figure 2.7 Configuring Benefit Plan Status

Now let us move on to the topic of groupings and the importance of infotype 0171 in the Benefits module.

2.3 First and Second Program Grouping

If you look back at Figure 2.4, you will notice the two fields of **First Program Grouping** and **Second Program Grouping**. The example shows the First Program Grouping as hourly and the Second Program Grouping as full time. Perhaps the plan eligibility is different for hourly and full-time employees than for hourly and part-time and salaried and full-time employees at this company. We will learn about the usage and significance of these groupings during configuration, but the key thing to remember is that groupings are used to determine eligibility for employees during the benefit enrollment and termination processes.

First Program Grouping

Hierarchically speaking, we will move down from Benefits area to a level for employee benefits eligibility.

Example

Within a Benefits area, you can further divide the employee population by the groupings.

You will be able to locate the configuration via menu path **Personnel Management • Benefits • Flexible Administration • Programs.**

These two groupings are the two dimensions provided by SAP for distinguishing between the employee populations to determine eligibility for benefits.

Example

Salaried, non-union employees have benefits that are different from hourly, union employees. Other examples include full-time and part-time employees having different types of benefits. In some cases, executive or manager-level employees also have different benefits. These and similar distinctions are managed by these two groupings.

The complexity is not in creating the groupings, but in designing your HR structures, which include personnel areas, sub-areas, employee groups, and sub-groups. Most SAP implementation projects do not address this aspect while designing HR structures, so you can end up having to redesign these structures.

Note

For more information on this, refer to the paper titled "Designing HR Structures" in *HR Expert's* October 2006 issue (http://*www.hrexpertonline.com*).

Look at the following example to help you better understand the groupings. In this example, an organization has a benefit plan whose features are based on the following attributes (the possible association with the HR structures is as shown in parentheses):

- Location of an employee (personnel area or sub-area)
- Whether an employee is full time or part time (employee group)
- Whether an employee is permanent or temporary (employee group or sub-group)
- Whether an employee is an active employee or retired (employment status or employee group)
- Which union the employee belongs to, given that, different unions have their own benefits or eligibility criteria (contract type)

You will need to create a two dimensional table using these criteria and align those to your HR structures. Figure 2.8 shows a simple configuration of the benefits grouping. Subsequently, the feature **BENGR,** as shown in Figure 2.9, will drive the defaults for the first program groupings into infotype 0171. This feature can be accessed using the **Feature** button shown in Figure 2.8. The sample decision logic in Figure 2.9 can be extended to drive the decision on a combination of elements from HR structures. Features can be accessed using Transaction PE03 and you can either use Pview mode or tree structure mode to look at them. In this case, we followed a Pview mode here.

1st Program Grouping	1st ProgrGroup.
EXEC	Executives
HRLY	Hourly Employees
RETI	Retirees
SALE	Salaried Exempt
SALN	Salaried Non-Exempt

Feature

Figure 2.8 Configuring Benefits Groupings

000080	10		D	PERSK
000090	10 U1			&BENGR=HRLY,
000100	10 U2			&BENGR=HRLY,
000110	10 U5			&BENGR=EXEC,
000120	10 U6			&BENGR=HRLY,
000130	10 U8			&BENGR=RETI,
000140	10 **			&BENGR=SAL,

Figure 2.9 BENGR Feature That Drives First Program Grouping

The concept of the Second Program Grouping is very similar to that of the first.

Second Program Grouping

As with the First Program Grouping, the Second Program Grouping gives the second dimension in infotype 0171 to decide the eligibility of employees. For example, a listing of full time in the First Program Grouping would be followed by a listing of salaried in the Second Program Grouping. Therefore, all full-time, salaried employees have different plan eligibility than do part-time, salaried employees. Part time and salaried would be another combination of First Program Grouping and Second Program Grouping. The configuration and feature **BSTAT** drives defaults for the Second Program Grouping. We will not repeat all of the steps for the Second Program Grouping, because they are so similar to the First Program Grouping, but in the next section, you will learn how these two groupings are tied together to decide the eligibility of plans through programs.

Define Benefit Programs

Now let us discuss the use of the First Program Grouping and Second Program Grouping to decide the eligibility of plans. The two dimensions — hourly/full time or salaried/full time — are used along with benefit plans. For example, the hourly/part-time combination is not eligible for dental plan, while only salaried full-time employees are eligible for pension plans.

Just as you did in the benefits area, you need to establish the relationship of the groupings with an employee through the features. We will use the HR structures in employee infotype 0001 to derive the defaults in features. At this point, you may be wondering how the benefit plans are determined based on these groupings. The IMG step using the menu path **Benefits • Flexible Administration • Programs • Define Benefits Programs** further processes these two groupings. Figure 2.10 shows the benefits -plan enrollment and termination as tied to the Salaried/Full Time Groupings. You need to be careful with this step because you will not be able to configure it unless you configure the following three areas:

- Plans
- Eligibility Rule
- Termination Rule

Later in this chapter, we will learn about eligibility and termination rules, but plan configuration is addressed in Chapter 3. We are explaining this step here because, logically, you need to know about the use of the groupings and the creation of the benefit groups with associated eligible plans. While you are creating a newly hired employee in the system using SAP's PA module, infotype 0171 should appear in a pop-up window with the appropriate defaults. Therefore, when the employee is processed for benefits enrollment, the eligible plans will be displayed as the configuration shown in Figure 2.10.

1st Program Gro SAL Salaried Employees
2nd Program Gro FULL Full time

Plan	Text	Elig.	Description	Term.	Description
401K	401K Savings Plan	IMED	Immediate	TRM1	Termination rule 1
AD&D	AD&D	IMED	Immediate	TRM1	Termination rule 1
DCAR	Dependent Care	IMED	Immediate	TRM1	Termination rule 1
DENT	Company Dental Plan	IMED	Immediate	TRM1	Termination rule 1
HCAR	Health Care Account	IMED	Immediate	TRM1	Termination rule 1
HCLB	Health Club Membership	IMED	Immediate	TRM1	Termination rule 1
LIF1	Dependent Life	IMED	Immediate	TRM1	Termination rule 1
LIFE	Company Life Insurance...	IMED	Immediate	TRM1	Termination rule 1
LIFS	Supplementary Life Insu...	IMED	Immediate	TRM1	Termination rule 1
LISP	Spousal Life	MMED	Married Immediate	TRM1	Termination rule 1

Figure 2.10 Assigning Plans to Program Groupings — Eligibility and Termination Rules

2.4 Managing Eligibility

After you have defined the First and Second Program Groupings, you might ask: What is the need for the Eligibility Groupings? Think about this as a further separation within the First and Second Program Groupings. Eligibility groups associate employees who have common characteristics that are relevant for benefits. The topic of eligibility will be divided further into groupings, variants, and rules in the IMG.

Eligibility Groupings

Within the same benefit grouping, you will be able to separate employees based on Eligibility groupings. To understand these, we will extend our example from the earlier section a step further. Let us take an example where infotype 0171 has salaried and full-time employees as First and Second Program Groupings. Among these employees, there are certain employees who are eligible for health club membership benefits; the Eligibility group will help you to identify them. We will call this grouping "EXEC." We have created a new group **EXEC** in Figure 2.11 using IMG menu path **Benefits • Flexible Administration • Program Grouping • Employee eligibility • Define Eligibility Groupings.**

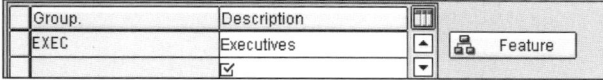

Figure 2.11 Creating an Eligibility Group

Clicking on the Feature button will lead you to **ELIGR**, where we have linked the appropriate personnel sub-area, based on the assumption that the HR structures allow us to find executive employees separately (using personnel sub-area) from this grouping. Figure 2.12 presents this feature. As mentioned before in the book, you will need to become very familiar with the many features in the Benefits module, so be sure to use the available documentation from SAP to learn about your many options.

```
000110 10           D BTRTL
000120 10 EXEC        &ELIGR=EXEC,
000130 10 ****        &ELIGR=SAL,
```

Figure 2.12 Feature ELIGR for Eligibility Grouping

We will now learn about eligibility variants, which in turn will be linked with eligibility groups.

Eligibility Variants

Before we go to Eligibility rules, there is an intermediate step for creating Eligibility variants. The variants have identifiers and descriptions associated with them. Why do you need these variants? Because in the next section, when we create the eligibility rule, you will see that we will be using a combination of groupings and variants. Variants are an additional dimension in SAP that offer you additional flexibility in your groupings.

Eligibility variant	Description
1 YR	Year Eligibility
30D	30 Day Eligibility
IMED	Immediate
MMED	Married Immediate

Figure 2.13 Creating Eligibility Variants

From the configuration shown in Figure 2.13, we will use a variant **IMED**. In this example, the executives are going to be immediately eligible for the benefits, so we have named it **IMED** for "immediate." The name itself has no significance unless you build some meaning into it.

Eligibility Rules

Eligibility rules tie the variant and the grouping together. You create Eligibility rules following the IMG menu path **Benefits • Flexible Administration • Program Grouping • Employee Eligibility • Define Eligibility Rule**. Figure 2.14 shows that the variant **IMED** and the grouping **EXEC** have been tied together through the rule.

The pyramid of Eligibility will be nested as: **Benefits area (US) • First Program Grouping (Salaried) • Second Program Grouping (Full Time) • Eligibility Grouping (EXEC-Executives) • Eligibility Variant (IMED-Immediate) • Eligibility Rule (IMED+EXEC)**. Therefore, employees who fit into all of these criteria will be immediately eligible for the appropriate benefit.

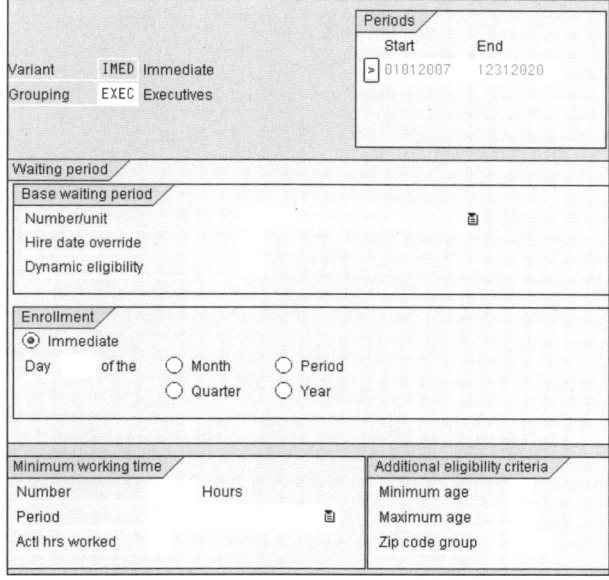

Figure 2.14 Creating Eligibility Rules

Any scenarios in which you need to manipulate the eligibility around enrollment time periods or work hours can be managed through this step. In Figure 2.14, you will also notice the field **Zip code group**, used because it helps to drive certain Location Based Eligibilities. This might occur if your personnel areas or sub-areas are at a higher level and you have within them restrictions of eligibility for a specific locality. Let us say that personnel area equals location and personnel sub-area equals departmental function, and certain geographical locations have special benefit plans. You will be able to use zip-code grouping through the IMG, menu path **Benefits • Flexible Adminis-**

tration Programs • Employee Eligibility • Zip Codes. These groupings can then associate the zip code for those geographical locations to exactly determine the locations and associated eligibility.

Dynamic Eligibility

Normally, some eligibility criteria in the benefits world are dependent on actual length of service or actual hours worked. These figures are not static and hence they are dynamic. Infotype 0041 (date specifications) plays an important role in deciding the Dynamic eligibility. This infotype allows you to create specific date types as shown in Figure 2.15.

Date type	Date type	Date indicator
U1	Hire Date	
U2	Adj. Service Date	
U3	Pension Date	
U4	Ben. Hire Date	
U5	First Working Date	

Figure 2.15 Date Specifications — Infotype 0041

Using the IMG menu path **Benefits • Flexible Administration • Programs • Employee Eligibility • Dynamic Eligibility** you can configure dynamic eligibility. You can take a certain date type from the date specifications infotype 0041 and then create conditions around it as shown in Figure 2.16.

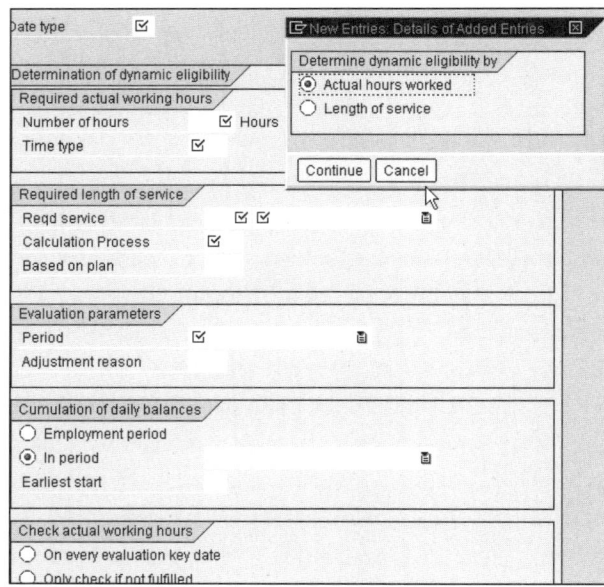

Figure 2.16 Dynamic Eligibility Conditions

In Chapter 3, we will discuss the plans configuration, and you will be able to put together some of the loose ends. Whenever you create conditions, there is always the question of where these conditions go. How does the system decide whether an employee is eligible for certain benefits based on these conditions? The groupings and the HR structures (infotype 0001) typically bring it all together with the configuration of plans.

2.5 Managing Dependent Eligibility

Unlike other functionality in HR, benefits functionality is always linked with dependents because of their coverage. The dependent-eligibility configuration has three aspects:

▶ Dependent eligibility variant
▶ Dependent eligibility rule
▶ Assigning the eligibility to the applicable benefit plan

Dependent Eligibility Variant

Prior to this configuration, you should have completed the configuration related to dependents (infotype 0021) as well as benefit plans. Therefore, the process can be repeated as you configure your plans.

Figure 2.17 shows the eligibility variant **HCLB** created for the health-club plan. You will reach the eligibility variant configuration by following the menu path **Benefits • Flexible Administration • Dependent/Beneficiary Eligibility • Define Dependent Eligibility Rule Variants**.

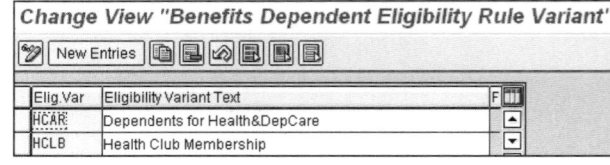

Figure 2.17 Dependent Eligibility Variant

Dependent Eligibility Rule

In the next step, we are using the dependent eligibility rule variant **HCLB** to create the rule as shown in Figure 2.18. Also note the student age limit column (titled **St.**). This will control the age to which the student dependents will be covered. The last column (**No max**.) is used to indicate disabled students for whom there will not be any age limit. At various places in the benefits configuration, you will come across the special provisions for disabled beneficiaries.

Figure 2.18 Dependent Eligibility Rule

In the last step, we will assign this rule to the appropriate plan. Figure 2.19 shows this assignment. The same steps can be followed for beneficiaries, and you will find the configuration along the same menu path in the IMG **Benefits • Flexible Adminsitration • Dependent/Beneficiary Eligibility**. Next we will discuss the termination status.

Similar to the Dependent eligibility rule, SAP also offers the Beneficiary eligibility rule. Since you will need to deal with beneficiaries for life and savings plans. Now we move on to termination status.

2.6 Termination

As with the other groupings, there are rules for benefits at termination. We complete the configuration under the IMG for **Flexible Administration** during the baseline configuration. And as with the enrollment stage, you need to know the benefits termination rules for the organizations.

The menu path **Benefits • Flexible Administration • Programs • Participation Termination** provides the configuration for managing the termination of an employees' coverage under their benefits plans.

Remember, there are three main elements to plan configuration: groupings, variants, and rules.

By now you should be familiar with these three areas, because you will notice that they are used for the entire configuration in SAP's Benefits module. Let us start our termination setup with the groupings discussion.

Termination Groupings

You will need different termination groupings here because some organizations enforce immediate terminations while others are more generous and offer coverage until the end of the month. In some cases, such as severance, organizations negotiate termination conditions with employees. While you are working with the termination groupings, you will need to extend your thinking a bit beyond the Benefits module to include:

- Personnel Administration Action Type (from infotype 0000)
- Personnel Administration Action Reason (from infotype 0000)

The employee termination/separation is carried out through PA actions. The action type and reason code drive the groupings, which we will explain shortly.

Figure 2.20 shows the creation of termination groupings using menu path **Benefits • Flexible Administration • Programs • Participation Termination • Define Termination Groupings.**

Figure 2.20 Define Termination Grouping

We have now created the new grouping and named it 15th, but the work is not complete until we manage the feature using the feature button. The name as such has no significance, but you should try and configure using meaningful naming standards. Figure 2.21 shows that in the feature, we are using an action type 01 to drive this grouping. In your configuration, you need to figure out the termination-related action types (voluntary or firing) and use it appropriately with this feature.

Figure 2.19 Assigning Dependent Eligibility to Benefit Plan

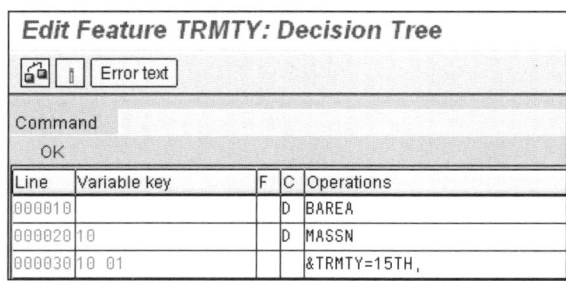

Figure 2.21 Action Type Usage in the Feature TRMTY

Termination Variant

Figure 2.22 shows the creation of the termination variant using the menu path **Benefits • Flexible Administration • Programs • Participation Termination • Define Termination Variants**. Just as with grouping, the name **15th** has no significance beyond following meaningful and standard naming convention.

Termination variant	Description
15TH	15th of month

Figure 2.22 Termination Variant

Termination Rules

In this last step, we will be linking the termination grouping from the first step with the termination variant from the second step to create a termination rule shown in Figure 2.23. The termination is on the 15th of month, as configured in the rule. If you recall our earlier discussion of Eligibility rules in Section 2.5, we followed a similar approach. We will therefore repeat the points about grouping and variants and how they link together in the rule.

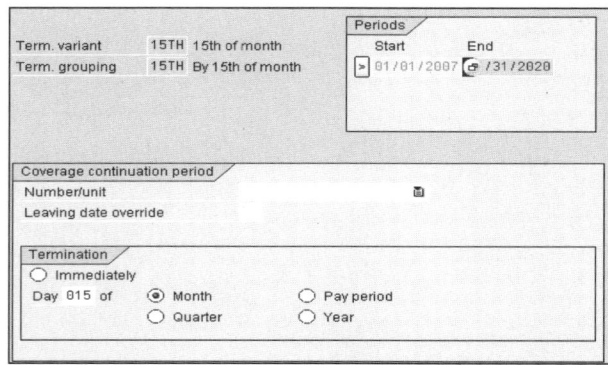

Figure 2.23 Defining Termination Rules

As seen in Figure 2.23, you can either terminate the employee's benefits immediately, or you can define a coverage continuity period. The Termination Monitor that we will run toward the end of this Chapter uses these rules to de-limit the benefits (i.e., Benefit infotypes 0167, 0168, etc.) are date de-limited. We will now discuss the adjustment reasons, which control the work- and life-event changes in benefits administration.

2.7 Adjustment Reasons

As we saw in Chapter 1, work and life events affect the benefits, and make it necessary for employees to make changes to their benefits choices. This topic is relevant here because, once again, you need this as part of your baseline configuration to get everything else working.

The life events and associated regulations allow the employee to make changes to the plans. infotype 0378, which can be accessed using PA Transactions PA30 or PA40, is the driver behind these life events. This infotype, for adjustment reasons, has a behind-the-scenes configuration that we will discuss in this section. The entire configuration is available through the IMG menu path **Benefits • Flexible Administration • Benefits Adjustment Reasons**.

The configuration can be roughly divided into three areas:
- Defining groupings
- Defining reasons
- Defining which plans can be changed and how they can be changed

Adjustment Reason Groupings

Why do we need to create yet another grouping? Because, for different types of employees, different permissions are required for changes to the plans. In Chapter 1, we learned that there is a business process around work and life events that allows employees to make changes to their plans.

> **Example**
>
> Childbirth would be a life event that required an employee to add a dependent to their health plans.

Figure 2.24 shows the commonly used grouping **FULL** for full-time employees. Typically, full-time employees are allowed to make changes to plans for their life events. A feature **EVTGR** allows you to associate the grouping with HR structures. It is clear that HR structures have significant impact on the employee benefit life events.

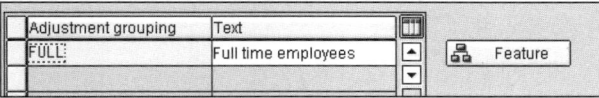

Figure 2.24 Adjustment Groupings

Figure 2.25 shows that for a benefits area with 10 decision criteria, the feature drives the grouping decision to **FULL**. Having learned the groupings for adjustment reasons, we will now explore the configuration of adjustment reasons.

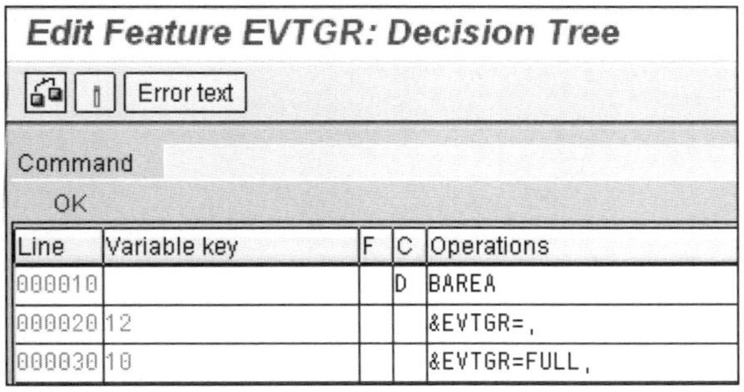

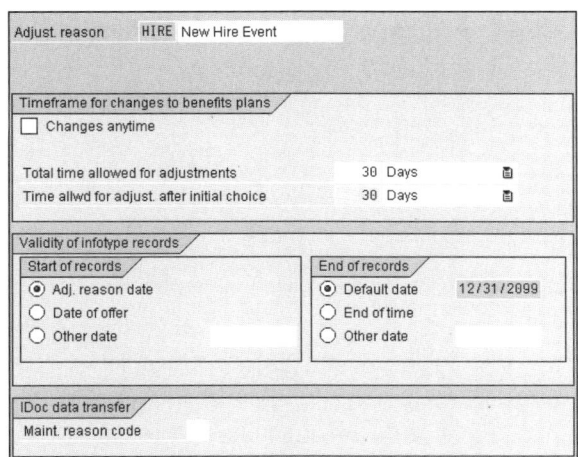

Figure 2.26 Configuring Adjustment Reasons

Linking Plan with Grouping and Reasons

The system needs to know which plan types are allowed to change for what groupings and the reason codes. Following the IMG path **Benefits • Flexible Administration • Benefits Adjustment Reasons • Define Adjustment Permissions** will allow you to link the different plans with adjustment groupings and reason codes. Figure 2.27 shows that the earlier reason code **HIRE** and grouping **FULL** are now linked with **Dental** plan type. This configuration decides whether the plan can be added to, changed, or deleted. In addition, coverage options as well as dependent changes are controlled.

Figure 2.25 Feature EVTGR for Adjustment Grouping

Adjustment Reasons

Using the IMG menu path **Benefits • Flexible Administration • Benefits Adjustment Reasons • Define Benefits Adjustment Reasons**, we will configure an adjustment reason related to a **New Hire Event**. Figure 2.26 shows the Adjustment Reason configuration screen. Note the field **Changes anytime**, in Figure 2.26, as well as the duration for adjustments in this screen. These fields will control whether the employee will be able to make changes after the life event.

Example
Typically, employees have 30 days to make changes.

How does the system know which plans the employees are allowed to change or create for their work or life events? The next step will explain this.

Example
For a life event like marriage or childbirth, the configuration will allow changes to dependent coverage.

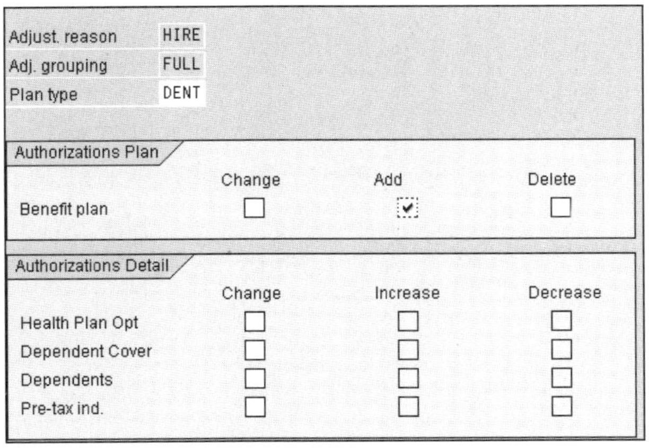

Figure 2.27 Linking Adjustment Groupings and Reasons

Let us step into the application side of the Benefits module to show you how this configuration comes together for the testing.

2.8 How It Works

So far, we have done a lot of configuration, so let us take a few minutes to work on checking the correctness of this configuration. Figure 2.28 shows infotype 0378 for an employee. This is based on the adjustment reasons configuration that you learned about previously.

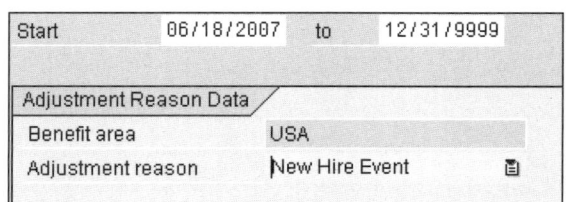

Figure 2.28 Infotype 0378 — Enrollment

As you are completing the maintenance of this infotype, the system will prompt you with the enrollment message, as shown in Figure 2.29. Subsequently, if you choose to go ahead, SAP will run the enrollment monitor as shown in Figure 2.30. We will not go into the details of the Enrollment Monitor just yet, but this explanation gives you an idea of how your configuration will work. The plans shown in Figure 2.30 are the plans that this employee is eligible to enroll in as a result of the adjustment reason code in infotype 0378, and the entire associated configuration.

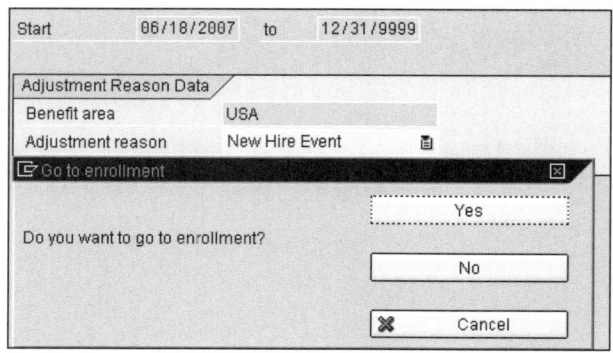

Figure 2.29 Prompt for Enrollment

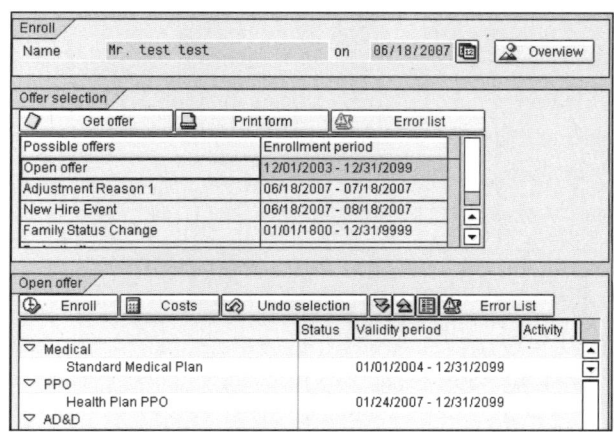

Figure 2.30 Enrollment Monitor

As with enrollment, let us take a look at termination so that you will understand the termination rules we discussed earlier. Figure 2.31 shows infotype 0378 with **Termination** as the reason for changes in the plan.

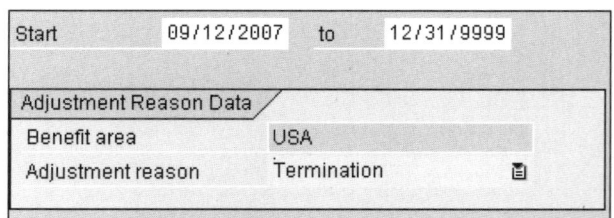

Figure 2.31 Infotype 0378 — Termination

When we run the Termination Monitor using the application menu path **Benefits • Termination,** we will get to the Termination Monitor screen as shown in Figure 2.32, and the system will allow us to terminate or de-limit the plans as configured by the termination rules. This is not a discussion of the Termination Monitor, just a recap of the impact of the configuration we have done so far.

Before we conclude this chapter, let us look at Figure 2.33. This shows the IMG screen for re-capping the baseline configuration that we covered in this chapter. We have covered the IMG nodes **Basic Settings** and **Flexible Administration** from this screen. We are now ready to move to the **Plans** node for the configuration.

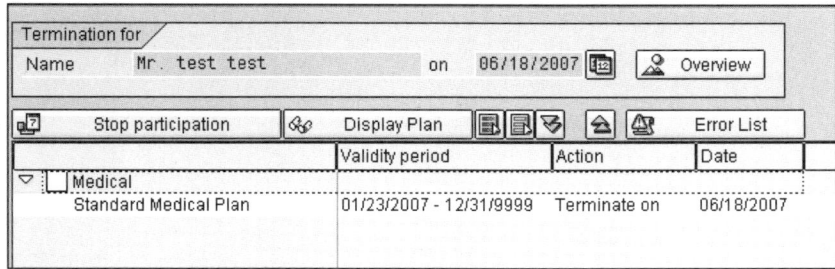

Figure 2.32 Termination Monitor

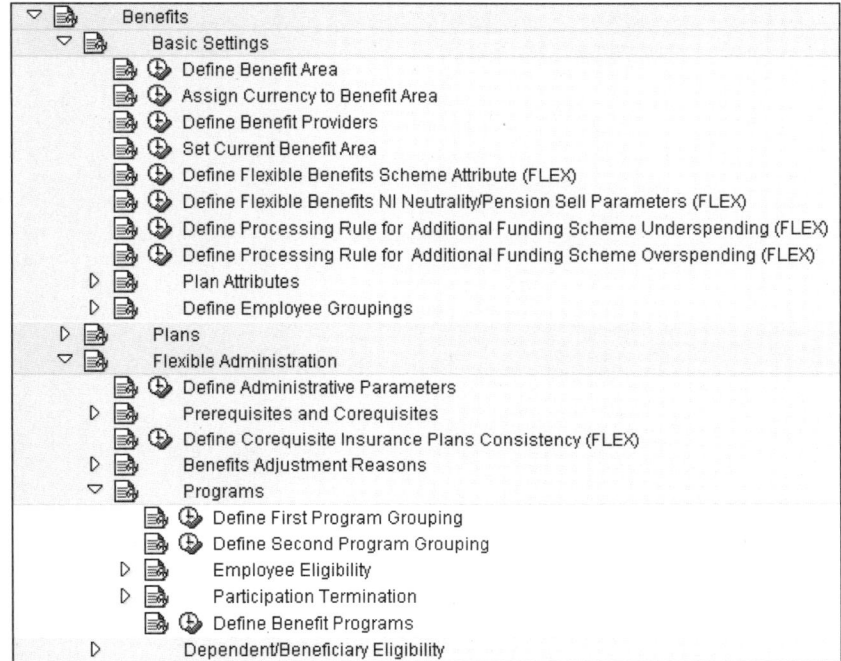

Figure 2.33 Recap of Baseline Configuration

2.9 Summary

A baseline configuration needs to be completed under the flexible administration section in the IMG. Although, the variants, groupings, and rules can get a little confusing at the beginning, they are logically related to each other. We need to keep our focus on the three phases of the employee benefits: life cycle-enrollment, changes due to life events, and termination. As we saw, the baseline, or preliminary configuration, logically follows these three phases and also helps us to understand the impact on the application.

In Chapter 3, we will explore the Plan Configuration in detail.

3 Plan Configuration

In this chapter, we will learn about the configuration of benefit plans. In addition to the various groupings and eligibility rules that we learned in earlier chapters, this chapter covers groupings related to employee eligibility that are used during plan configurations.

As we learned in Chapter 1, benefit plans are categorized as Health, Insurance, Savings, Flexible Spending Accounts (FSAs), Miscellaneous, and Stocks. Configuration of these plans allows us to control the cost, coverage, and other attributes. The plans are linked with deduction wage types from payroll, and the benefit providers and HR payees for sending the remittance and employee data. We will start with the employee groupings offered by SAP to control the costs, coverage and criteria for employees. These groupings drive the eligibility for an employee related to enrollment in a particular benefit plan. SAP's Benefits module contains many different types of groupings; in the last chapter we covered the program groupings, while this chapter starts the discussion with employee groupings.

3.1 Defining Employee Groupings

Benefit plans normally have different costs, such as employee cost, employer cost, and provider cost. These amounts can vary based on certain employee groupings.

> **Example**
> There is a grouping based on age, and the life insurance amounts can differ by the age.

The discussion in this section is around these groupings. We will learn the different ways in which the groupings can be used to drive the costs for plans. Please note that these groupings are used in the plan configuration, so you will need to loop back to the configuration between plans and the groupings in this chapter. Let us start by defining the employee criteria groups.

Define Employee Criteria Groups
There are three types of criteria groupings:
- Salary
- Age
- Seniority

However, there is also a second dimension to these groupings called Parameter group. Each of the above is related to the Parameter group. Why is the Parameter group necessary? Before we answer this question, let us discuss what the Parameter group is.

Parameter Group
Using the menu path **Benefits • Basic Settings • Define Employee Groupings • Define Employee Criteria Groups • Define Parameter Groups,** we can define the Parameter group as shown in Figure 3.1. We have created a Parameter group **PAR1**.

Parameter group	Description	Currency
PAR1	Parameter Group 1	

Figure 3.1 Creating the Parameter Group

In the next step, we will configure a sample Salary group to show the linkage between Parameter group and Salary group.

3 Plan Configuration

Salary Group

Figure 3.2 shows the Salary groups **SAL1** and **SAL2** created under Parameter group **PAR1**.

Parameter group	PAR1	Parameter Group 1		
Salary group	Description	Low value	High value	Cur
SAL1	Salary Slab 1	25,000.00	49,999.00	
SAL2	Salary Slab 2	50,000.00	99,999.00	

Figure 3.2 Salary Groups

As we get to the details of benefit plans, we will be using the Parameter group PAR1 with its associated second dimension of Salary group SAL1.

Age Group

Figure 3.3 shows the different age groups **AGE1** and **AGE2** that are created under parameter group **PAR1**. Similar to salary group, we have now added another group under **PAR1**, which is based on age range.

Parameter group	PAR1	Parameter Group 1	
Age Group	Description	Minimum age	Maximum age
AGE1	Age Group 1	21	49
AGE2	Age Group 2	50	65

Figure 3.3 Age Groups

> **Example**
> For insurance plans, we can use age-based costs.

The next group is seniority.

Seniority Groups

Figure 3.4 shows different seniority groups **SEN1** and **SEN2** created under parameter group **PAR1**. You can create multiple groups for age, salary, or seniority under one parameter group or you can create multiple parameter groups for each age or salary group. This will be clarified later, when we discuss the configuration of plans in more detail.

Parameter group	PAR1	Parameter Group 1	
Seniority group	Description	Lowest value	Max.value
SEN1	Seniority Slab 1	5	9
SEN2	Seniority Slab 2	10	15

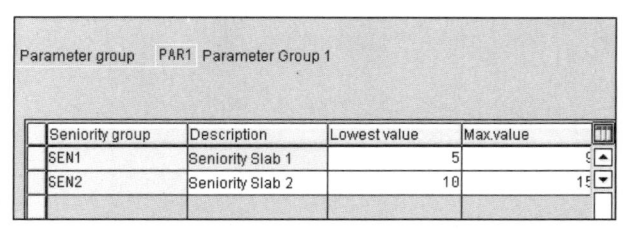

Figure 3.4 Seniority Groups

Now imagine a situation where one plan requires a certain age group range (example: 29-55) and another plan requires an age group range that is overlapping (example: 40-61). Because you cannot create an overlapping range, you will need to create a separate parameter group. Therefore, SAP has provided you with the second dimension of parameter groups called *Cost groupings* for health plans, *Coverage groupings* for insurance plans, and *Contribution groupings* for savings plans. Let us start the discussion first with Cost groupings.

Define Cost Groupings

Cost groupings are used to drive costs through cost variants and rules. Figure 3.5 shows the Cost groupings **COS1** and **COS2** created using the IMG path **Benefits • Basic Settings • Define Employee Groupings • Define Cost Groupings**.

Cost grouping	Description	
COS1	Cost Grouping 1	Feature
COS2	Cost Grouping 2	

Figure 3.5 Cost Groupings

The best part of benefits configuration is always the features. If you click on the **Feature** button in Figure 3.5, it will bring up feature **CSTV1**. This feature allows you to make a decision about different Cost groupings based on the HR structure. As mentioned in Chapter 2, the HR structures play an extremely important role in benefits configuration. For example, if we want to drive different costs by location (personnel area, sub-area) or by type of employee (employee group, sub-group), we can use this feature to drive appropriate groupings.

The health plan configuration illustrates the usage of these groupings. We will discuss the particular configuration later in this chapter, but if you are curious you can follow the IMG menu path **Benefits • Plans • Health Plans**

- **Define Cost Rules,** to see the cost grouping field while creating those rules. You will notice that these groupings are applicable to health plans. Figure 3.6 shows the feature available when we click on the feature button from Figure 3.5. For a decision based on **Benefits Area SB** and employee sub-group U4, the feature returns the value of **CSTV1** for the cost rule.

Line	Variable key	F	C	Operations
000090	SB		D	PERSK
000100	SB U4			&CSTV1=CST1,
000110	SB U1			&CSTV1=CST2,
000120	SB **			&CSTV1=CST2,

Figure 3.6 Feature CSTV 1 Decision Tree

Defining Coverage Groupings

This concept is very similar to what we learned earlier with respect to cost groupings. If we want to differentiate coverage based on certain criteria, we can create different groupings and then use the associated feature to drive the decision.

> **Example**
> Employees in a manufacturing plant have higher coverage than those in the corporate office.

Figure 3.7 shows the coverage groupings COV1 and COV2.

Coverage grouping	Cover.grouping text	
COV1	Manufacturing	Feature
COV2	Office	

Figure 3.7 Coverage Groupings

Figure 3.8 shows that the two locations (personnel areas in HR structures) drive the decision to use the different coverage groupings. Personnel area 3000 will use coverage grouping **COV1**.

Line	Variable key	F	C	Operations
000010			D	WERKS
000020	3000			&COVGR=COV1,
000030	3001			&COVGR=COV2,
000040	****			&COVGR=COV2,

Figure 3.8 Feature COVGR

Now we need to jump to the insurance plan configuration to see how these groupings are used. We will cover the particular configuration later in this chapter, but for now you can follow the IMG menu path **Benefits • Plans • Insurance Plans • Define Cost Rules,** and you will see the use of the Coverage Grouping field while creating those rules. You will notice that these groupings are applicable to insurance plans as the word "coverage" suggests. Just as the coverage groupings are relevant for insurance plans, the contribution groupings are relevant for 401k (savings) plans.

> **Note**
> We use cost groupings for health plans, coverage groupings for insurance plans, and contribution groupings for savings plans.

Employee Contribution Grouping

The concept behind groupings and their associated features is similar to the one we discussed earlier. In this case, the employee contribution groupings are applicable for savings plans. Let us create the groupings followed by a feature to drive the decision based on HR structures or other elements available in **Feature**. These groupings are used to drive different employee (EE) contribution amounts to plans. Figure 3.9 shows the two groupings **CNT1** and **CNT2**. Figure 3.10 shows the feature **EECGR** associated with these groupings. This example uses the First Program Grouping field to drive the decision. In the example in Figure 3.10, the First Program Grouping **FULL** will follow EE contribution grouping **CNT1**. The IMG menu path **Benefits • Basic Settings • Define Employee Groupings • Define Employee Contribution Groupings** will lead you to this configuration. The groupings will be used later, when we discuss savings plans.

EE contr. grouping	Text
CNT1	Cntr Grpg 1
CNT2	Cntr Grpg 2

Feature

Figure 3.9 Employee Contribution Groupings

OK

Line	Variable key	F	C	Operations
000010			D	BENGR
000020	FULL			&EECGR=CNT1,
000030	PART			&EECGR=CNT2,

Figure 3.10 Feature EECGR

Now that we have covered employee contributions, we will discuss the employer contribution groupings. In 401k plans, you will normally have employee as well as employer contributions to the plan.

Define Employer Contribution Grouping

These are similar to the employee contribution grouping, and the feature **ERCGR** is used. These groupings are used to drive differences in employer contribution amounts based on the decision tree in the feature.

We need to jump to the savings plan configuration to see the usage of these groupings, but not until later in this chapter. However, if you are curious you can follow the IMG menu path **Benefits • Plans • Savings Plans • Define Employee Contribution Rules / Define Employer Contribution Rules** and see the employee contribution or employer contribution field while creating those rules. These groupings are applicable to savings plans.

Now let us move to the configuration of benefit plans and discuss the use of these groupings. It may be a good idea to re-read the information on different groupings when we refer to them in discussing configuration of related plans in the sections to follow. As we get to the plan configurations and start using these groupings, you will get a more complete picture, and revisiting the topic on groupings may be helpful.

3.2 Health Plans

The configuration of health plans starts with the general data for the plans, followed by configuration of cost variants and rules. Health plans share the following characteristics:

- They have providers.
- They offer options for family coverages.
- They can have different choices based on deductible or differences such as HMO, PPO, dental, etc.
- They will have different costs depending upon the choice of the employee as well as other groupings that we discussed earlier.
- Please refer to the standard SAP documentation (*https://help.sap.com*) if you want to learn more about the conceptual details about health, dental, or other medical plans. We will start configuring a health plan with general data followed by the cost-related configuration. The structure that we use to learn health plan configuration will be very similar to what we used for insurance, savings, and miscellaneous plans.

Plan General Data

Figure 3.11 illustrates the general-data step. You will notice that the fields **Plan Type**, **Plan Status**, and **Provider**, which we discussed in Chapter 2, are now used in the plan. The IMG path **Benefits • Plans • Health Plans • Define Health Plan General Data** is used to access this step. The **Pre-tax allowed checkbox** is used to manage the pre-tax deduction for health plans, which means the health plan deduction is taken from the employee's pay before taxes are calculated.

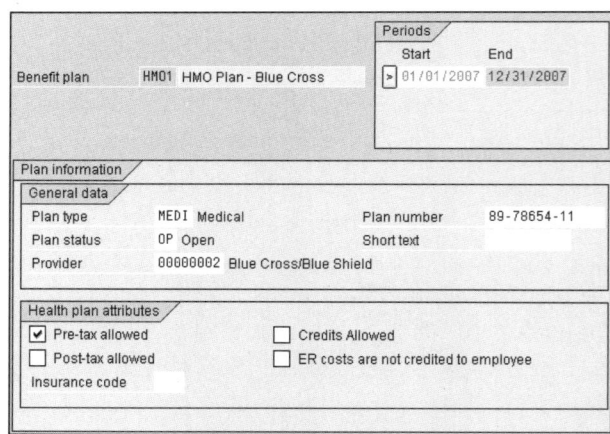

Figure 3.11 Health Plan General Data

Options for Health Plans

The scenarios with options are based on differentiators such as deductibles or co-pays. Remember that the options will affect the cost of the plan. Figure 3.12 shows different options that are configured for **HMO1** plan.

Example

In Figure 3.12, the higher-deductible plans may be cheaper.

IMG path **Benefits • Plans • Health Plans • Define Options for Health Plans** is used to access this step.

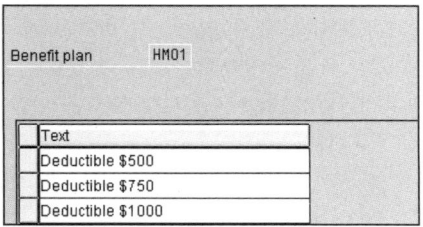

Figure 3.12 Options for Health Plans

You will get an opportunity to see how this configuration is tied together for an employee later in this chapter.

Dependent Coverage Options

Figure 3.13 shows the standard example of dependent coverage options with minimum and maximum limits. Some teams also follow the standard of **EE+1**, **EE+2**, etc. instead of letters as shown in Figure 3.13. The IMG path is **Benefits • Plans • Health Plans • Define Dependent Coverage Options**. In this step, you create Employee Only (**EE**), Employee + Spouse (**EE+S**), Employee + Family (**EE + F**) and similar dependent coverage options.

EE	Self		
EE+C	Self + Child	1	1
EE+F	Self + Family	2	20
EE+S	Self + Spouse	1	1

Figure 3.13 Dependent Coverage Options

Defining Cost Variants and Rules

The two steps that we will discuss here are the most important steps in the configuration of plans. These steps also use the different groupings that we learned earlier in Section 3.1.

Define Cost Variants

In this first step, you will need to create a cost variant that will then be used in the next step for creating the rule. Figure 3.14 illustrates the following tasks:

- Used parameter group **PAR1** (refer to sub-section Parameter Group)
- Check-marked **salary**, **age**, and cost **grouping**
- Defined cut-off days for salary and age, because those are check-marked

The IMG path **Benefits • Plans • Health Plans • Define Cost Variants** is used to access this step.

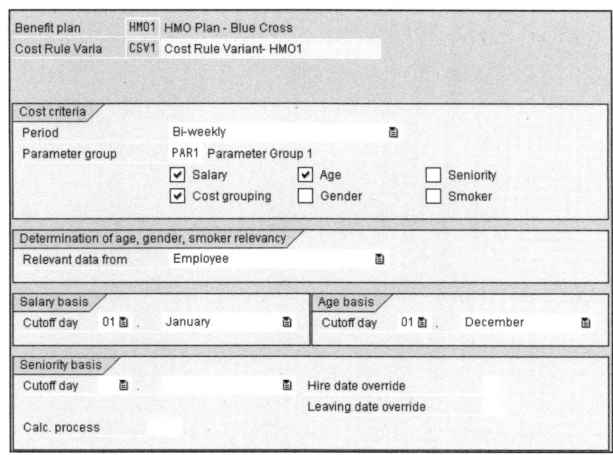

Figure 3.14 Define Cost Variant

In the next step, we will use this variant to create a rule. The variant brings the different dimensions based on groupings, and the rule generates the cost for the combination of those groupings.

Define Cost Rules

Using the cost variant, let us create a cost rule as shown in Figure 3.15. The system will allow you to drop down and pick the values related to salary, age, and cost groupings. This is because we used them in a cost variant earlier, and we configured the different groupings in Section 3.1 of this chapter. The values **SAL1**, **AGE1**, and **COS1** come from our previous configuration steps. For the combination of all these groupings, the costs are as entered in the lower portion of screen.

Example

If an employee fits into salary grouping **SAL1**, age grouping **AGE1**, and cost grouping **COS1**, then the employee will be paying $55.17 for the **HMO1** plan.

You do not have to use the groupings. The groupings are not meant to make the configuration complicated, but to give tremendous flexibility, if the employee population needs to be divided by these types of groupings. IMG path **Benefits • Plans • Health Plans • Define Cost Rules** is used to access this step.

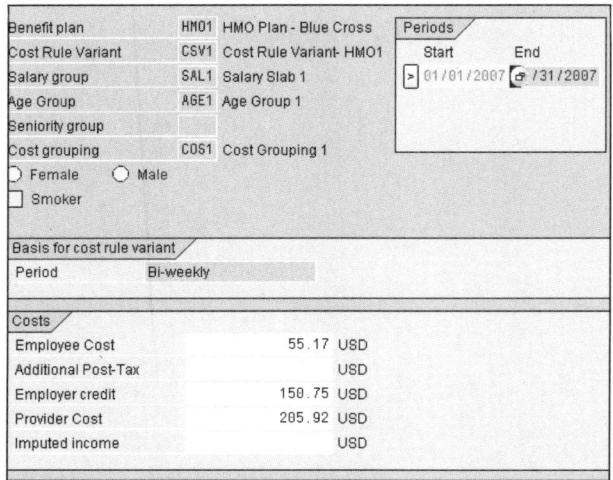

Figure 3.15 Define Cost Rule

Clearly, there can be more than one cost rule with a cost variant. As seen in the beginning of Chapter 2, all configuration takes place within a benefits area; therefore, if you have multiple benefits areas with multiple plans, the configuration needs to be repeated for each benefits area.

Managing Plan Attributes

For each plan, you need to bring the options, dependent coverage, and cost variants together. Therefore, when an employee chooses the options with dependents, the appropriate costs will be pulled. The IMG path **Benefits • Plans • Health Plans • Assign Health Plan Attributes** is used to access this step. Figure 3.16 shows the health plan attribute assignment to the plan **HMO1** in the example.

Figure 3.16 Assign Health Plan Attributes

In Chapter 4, we will discuss the application side of SAP Benefits module. However, below are some simple steps to test your configuration.

Testing the Configuration

It is always a good idea to run the unit tests after you complete the configuration, especially because the Benefits module has different configuration concepts, such as variants, groupings, and rules. For example, after completing the health plan configuration, we will use infotype 0167 and check if the pull-down options and the costs match the configuration that was carried out before. In Figure 3.17, you can see the options in a pull down menu; these are the values we configured in Figure 3.12.

We will learn more about this version and how to check enrollment in Chapter 4. For now, let us move to insurance plans.

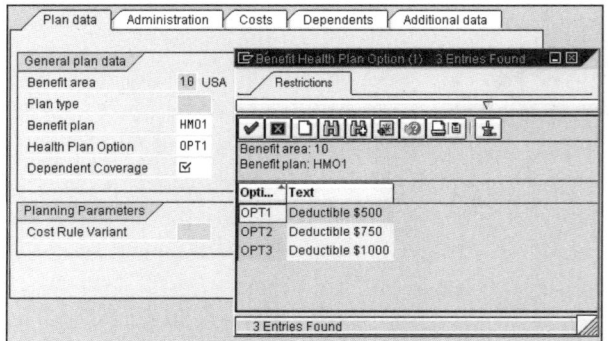

Figure 3.17 Testing infotype 0167- Health Plan

3.3 Insurance Plans

Life insurance coverage for employees or in some cases for their dependents is one of the important benefits that many organizations offer. When you think of insurance plans, some of the obvious characteristics are:

- They have providers
- They offer coverage based on amounts to employee or dependents
- Insurance rates differ by age, smoker, or non-smoker status
- Group term life insurance (GTLI) has tax implications

3.3 Insurance Plans

> **Note**
> Those of you interested in learning about imputed income or integration with payroll can refer to the SAP PRESS book, *Practical SAP US Payroll*.

In health plans, the focus was about costs as well as eligibility. In Insurance Plans, the focus will be around coverage because we are discussing life insurance. Similar to health plans, we will start with general data configuration.

Plan General Data

We can use the IMG path **Benefits • Plans • Insurance Plans • Define Insurance Plan General Data** to access this step the same way that we did with health plans. Figure 3.18 shows the general data for insurance plans. Please note that the **Imputed income** box is checked for this plan.

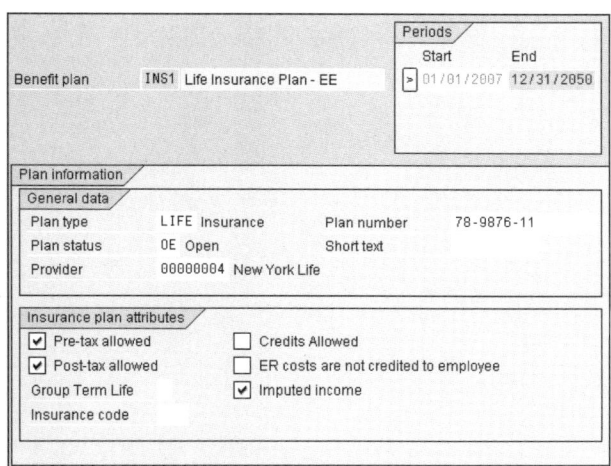

Figure 3.18 Insurance Plans General Data

Define Coverage Variants and Rules

The theory of variants followed by rules is very similar to our earlier discussions in this chapter. First we will create a variant and then use it in a rule. Because we are discussing insurance plans, we need to talk about coverage.

Define Coverage Variant

Please refer to the earlier cost-variant discussion and Figure 3.14. Now, if you look at Figure 3.19, you will notice that we have used the same Parameter group. Because insurance coverage normally depends on age, let us use the same age group. Note that the cut-off day for the age is December 31st. The IMG path to get to the coverage variant is **Benefits • Plans • Insurance Plans • Define Coverage Variants**.

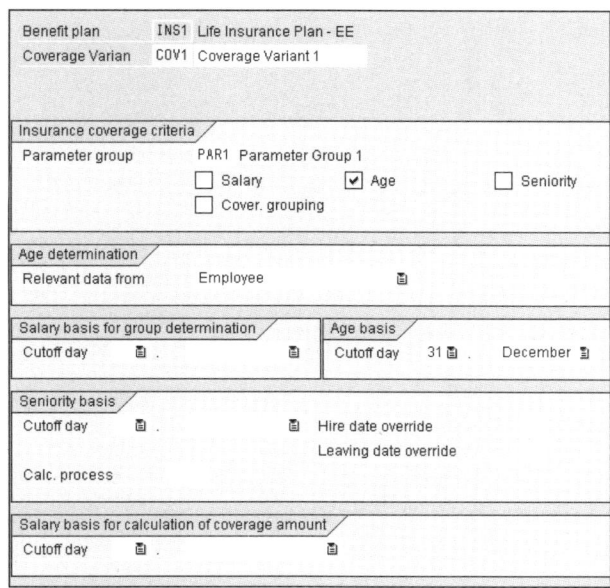

Figure 3.19 Define Coverage Variant

Define Coverage Rule

Using the coverage variant, we will create a coverage rule. Figure 3.20 shows the coverage rule. Because we only check the marked age group in the variant, the rule uses age group **AGE1**. The IMG path to get to this configuration is **Benefits • Plans • Insurance Plans • Define Coverage Rules**.

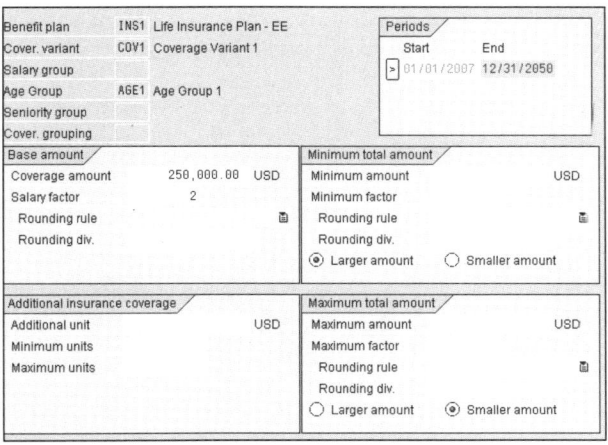

Figure 3.20 Coverage Rule

3 Plan Configuration

Define Cost Variants and Rules

As we saw earlier in health plans, we will need to create cost variants and cost rules for insurance plans. These will help us to determine the costs for the plans. Similar to coverage variants and rules, the menu for cost variants and rules is found under **Benefits • Plans • Insurance Plans**.

Define Cost Variants

The cost variants are defined for a plan and therefore are plan specific. Figure 3.21 shows a cost variant for the insurance plan. Costs are typically higher for smokers in the case of insurance plans. Therefore, you will normally have variants where the smoker box can be checked as in Figure 3.21.

Define Cost Rules

We will now use the variant to create the cost rule as shown in Figure 3.22. The fields in this figure are different than the cost rule we saw for health plans in Figure 3.15. The equation **Cost = (Coverage Amount/Base Unit) * Cost Factor** is illustrated in Figure 3.22.

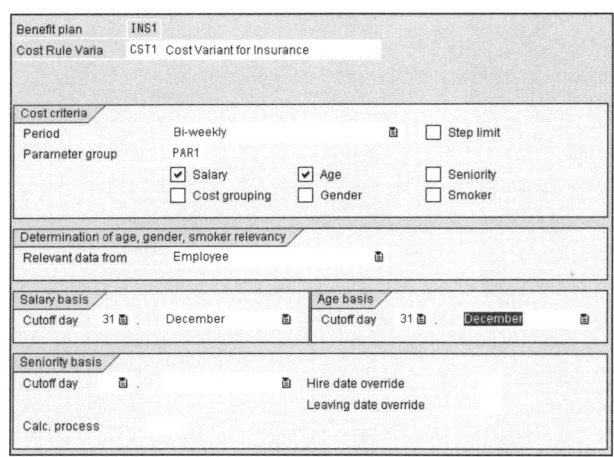

Figure 3.21 Cost Variant for Insurance Plan

> **Example**
>
> In Figure 3.22, for a coverage amount of $100,000, the cost for the employee will be $20.00.

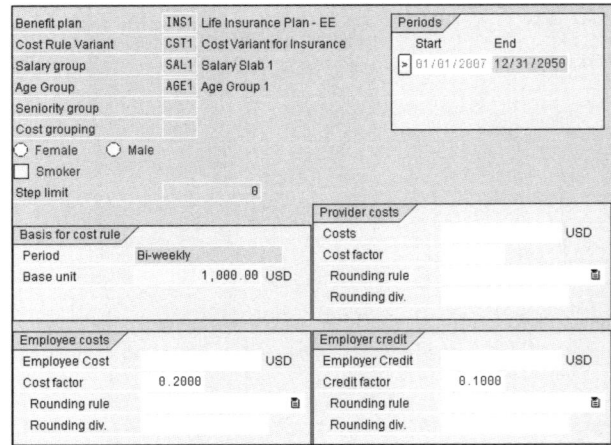

Figure 3.22 Insurance Plan Cost Rule

Managing Plan Attributes

In this step, you create different coverage options by attaching the coverage variant and cost variant as shown in Figure 3.23. The menu path in IMG to assign the attributes is **Benefits • Plans • Insurance Plans • Assign Insurance Plan Attributes**.

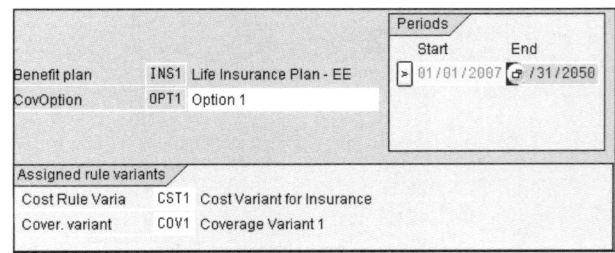

Figure 3.23 Manage Plan Attributes

What is an Imputed Income?

With insurance plans, you will always discuss the imputed income. If an employer extends group life insurance coverage of more than $50,000, then an imputed income is calculated per Internal Revenue Service (IRS) rate tables and is subject to Federal Insurance Contribution Act (FICA) taxes. The imputed income will appear in the pay stub and is normally dependent on two aspects: age groups and associated calculation factors, both of which are mandated by the IRS. IMG menu path **Benefits • Plans • Insurance Plans • Imputed Income for Selected Benefits** will lead you to configuration of these two aspects. Figure 3.24 shows the factors associated with age groups.

Age Group	Description	Start Date	End Date	Factor
09	Age Under 24	07/01/1999	12/31/9999	0.0
10	Age 25-29	07/01/1999	12/31/9999	0.0
11	Age 29 and Under	01/01/1900	06/30/1999	0.0
12	Age 30-34	07/01/1999	12/31/9999	0.0
13	Age 35-39	07/01/1999	12/31/9999	0.0
14	Age 40-44	07/01/1999	12/31/9999	0.1
15	Age 45-49	07/01/1999	12/31/9999	0.1
16	Age 50-54	07/01/1999	12/31/9999	0.2
17	Age 55-59	07/01/1999	12/31/9999	0.4
18	Age 60-64	07/01/1999	12/31/9999	0.6
19	Age 65-69	07/01/1999	12/31/9999	1.2
20	Age 70 and Above	07/01/1999	12/31/9999	2.0
5	Infants-Kids	12/06/2006	12/07/2007	0.5

Figure 3.24 Age Groups for Imputed Income

Figure 3.25 shows the technical wage type **/BT1** in payroll results table RT. This wage is created for imputed income calculation.

```
1 /001 Valuation b01              23.67
1 /002 Valuation b01              23.67
1 /003 Valuation b01              23.67
1 /BER Benefits ER01                          518.53
1 /BT1 EE GTLI Tax01                            2.22
1 1001 Hourly rate01              23.67
1 1200 Regular wor01              23.67  80.00  1,893.60
1 2317 Dental Empl01    B 01                    3.33
1 2320 Basic Life 01    B 04                    0.89
```

Figure 3.25 Imputed Income Wage Type

3.4 Savings Plans

The savings plans are most commonly referred to as 401k plans in the U.S. They require configuration similar to health and insurance plans. However, insurance plans had their own differentiators in configuration compared to health plans. Similarly, the savings plans have their own unique configuration aspects. Some obvious characteristics of savings plans are as follows:

- They are managed by financial companies
- Employee as well as employer contribute to the plan
- IRS-mandated annual pre-tax and post-tax contribution limits apply
- Employees choose to distribute the contribution to different investments or mutual funds
- Depending upon age, additional catch-up contribution is permitted

We will start the configuration with general plan data, similar to our earlier discussion of health and insurance plans.

Plan General Data

Figure 3.26 shows the plan general data for a savings plan named 401k. Please note the **457** and **403(b)** plan checkboxes are kept for public-sector and higher-education implementations. The qualified plan checkbox in this figure helps the system to check the annual pre-tax limits for benefit plans. You can use more than one 401k plan, and the combined annual limits can be checked during the deduction processing.

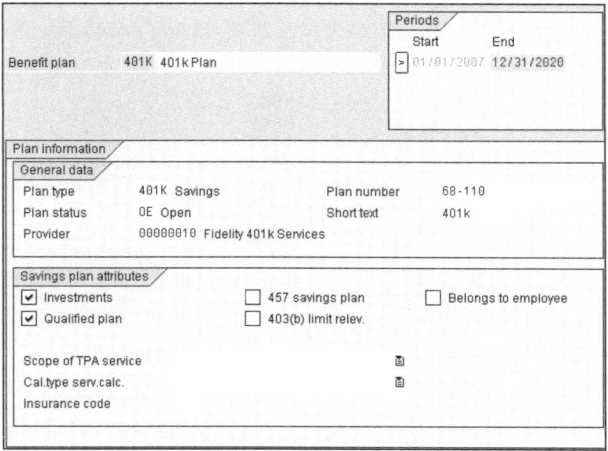

Figure 3.26 Savings Plan General Data

We will discuss the cost variants and rules for savings plans as we did in case of health and insurance plans.

Employee Contribution Variants and Rules

By now, you should be very familiar with the concepts of variant and rule and how they are used in the plans. We have seen examples for both health and insurance plans. The role of variants for savings plan is very similar to that in earlier examples. We will first discuss the employee contribution, then discuss the employer contribution in the next sub-section. Because we are dealing with the savings plan, the word "contribution" should make sense.

Define Contribution Variant

As we said earlier, variants are plan dependent. Therefore, when you configure the contribution variant, you configure it for a particular plan. Figure 3.27 shows the contribution variant **SAV1** for the savings plan that we created in earlier steps. The name **SAV1** has no significance as such and we are trying to effectively use the four-character namespace. Unlike the examples in health

3 Plan Configuration

and insurance plans, we are not using any Parameter groups for the configuration. The only configuration we are using in this figure is around beginning of the month for employee contribution as shown by the **Day** field at the end of the screen. The IMG menu path **Benefits • Plans • Savings Plans • Define Employee Contribution Variants** will lead you to the configuration.

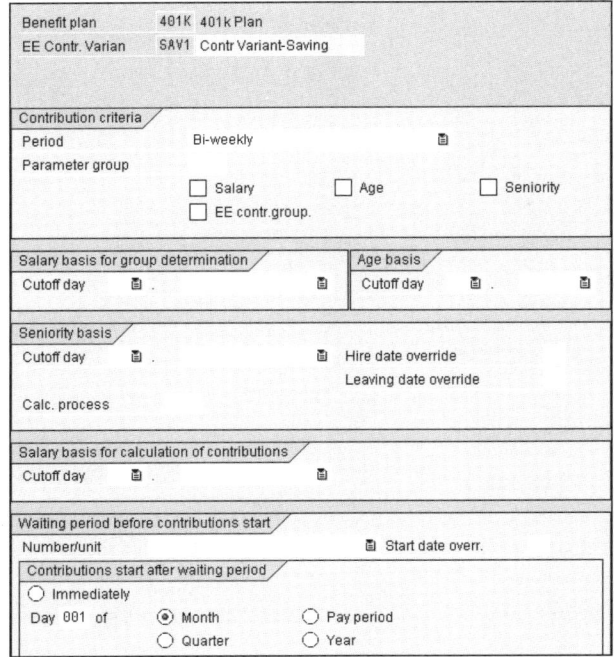

Figure 3.27 Employee Contribution Variant

Define Employee Contribution Rules

For a combination of plan and variant, create a rule as shown in example in Figure 3.28. Because we did not use the parameter group while creating the variant, the fields related to age, and salary grouping do not apply to our example. Because the contribution rule definition has a lot of fields and information, they are separated into Figures 3.28 and 3.29. Figure 3.28 shows that the contribution rule allows an employee to contribute both percentage and the dollar amounts. The **Pre-tax** and **Post-tax** checkboxes are used to allow the contribution for both pre-tax limits as well as roll-over to post-tax limits. In case of savings plans, SAP allows you to use the flexibility for bonus amounts at various places. Therefore, you will notice that you have separate flags for **Bonus** contributions in Figure 3.28. The bonus runs in SAP Payroll relate to infotype 0267 based on off-cycle runs. IMG menu path

Benefits • Plans • Savings Plans • Define Employee Contribution Rules will lead you to the configuration of contribution rules.

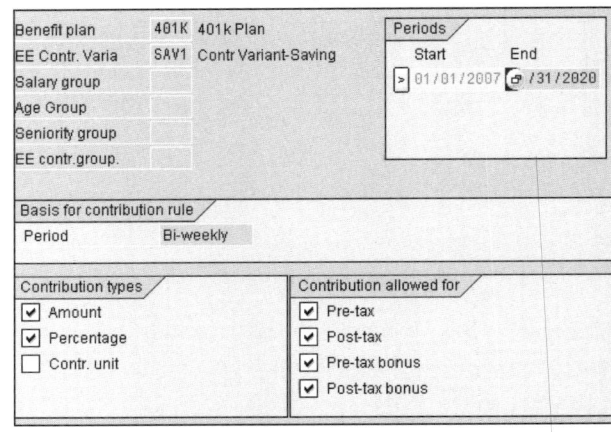

Figure 3.28 Employee Contribution Rule — Types and Tax Categories

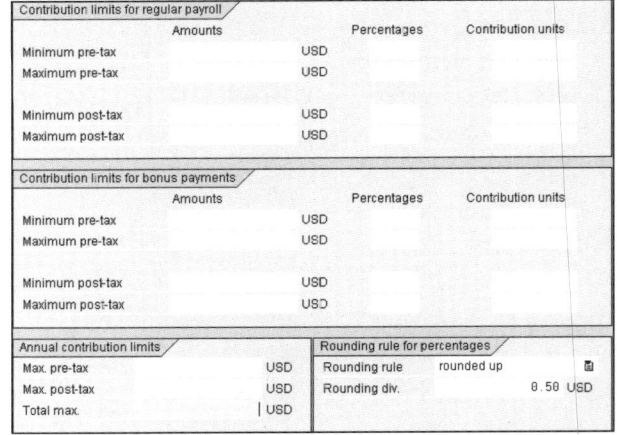

Figure 3.29 Employee Contribution Rule — Contribution Limits

In the later part of the contribution rule definition, as shown in Figure 3.29, we define the contribution limits with **Minimum** and **Maximum** values. Once again, these can be defined separately for **Regular Payroll** as well as **Bonus Payroll** as shown in Figure 3.29. Most of the time, you will not need to use the portion of rule definition shown in Figure 3.29. The annual pre-tax and post-tax limits in SAP are checked from values in a constant table. If you follow the IMG menu path **Payroll USA • Benefits Integration • Constants for Benefits Processing • Maintain Constants for Savings Plans,** you can get to the Constants Table T511P, which maintains the annual pre-tax limit ($15,500 in year 2007). In addition, this configuration helps you to set up the age-based catch-up contribution limit value ($5,000 in year 2007 and $6,000 in year 2008). You will find the catch-up contribution wage type linkage using the IMG menu path **Payroll USA • Benefits Integration • Set up Catchup Contribution**.

> **Note**
> Employees in the US who have reached the age of 50 can contribute more to retirement accounts under the catch-up provisions of 2002 legislation.

After you learn the employee contribution variant and rule, the employer contribution configuration is almost an exact replica. Everything is similar, except that the configuration is for the employer contribution instead of employee contribution. IMG menu path **Benefits • Plans • Savings Plans • Define Employer Contribution Variants** will lead you to the configuration of contribution variants for an employer. Followed by this node in IMG, you will have the employer rule configuration node. The screens will be the same as shown in Figures 3.28 and 3.29.

Manage Plan Atrributes
IMG menu path **Benefits • Plans • Savings Plans • Assign Savings Plan Attributes** will take us to configuration as shown in Figure 3.30.

Figure 3.30 Savings Plan Attributes

We now link the employee contribution variant as well as employer contribution variant from earlier steps to a savings plan. Therefore, when we use this plan for an employee, the appropriate rules will be applied. In the next step, we will create a vesting rule. Should you decide to use the rule for this plan, you need to come back to this step in IMG and attach that vesting rule to the plan.

Define Vesting Rule
Many companies require that employees work for a certain numbers of years with the company before they can claim the employer portion of the savings plan. Typically, companies adopt a four- to five-year year period with a percentage vested that the employee is entitled to each year. Figures 3.31 and 3.32 show the creation of **Vesting Rules** using IMG path **Benefits • Plans • Savings Plans • Define Vesting Rule**. Figure 3.31 has a rule **VET1** that uses a **Hire-Date Override**. The date type used in the configuration of rule is from infotype 0041 date specifications. Figure 3.32 shows that 25% will be vested each year, and if the employee stays with the company for four years the employer contribution will be fully vested. The rule created in Figure 3.31 is used in Figure 3.32.

Figure 3.31 Vesting Rule Definition for rule VET1

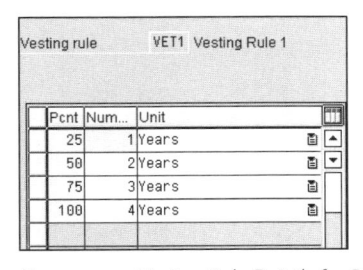

Figure 3.32 Vesting Rule Details for Rule VET1

Managing Investments for Savings Plans
Most companies hand over this functionality to funds-management companies. The SAP Benefits module sends the deductions via interface to the funds-management companies, and employees normally are given access to the Web-based tools to choose the funds and distribute payroll 401k deductions to these funds. SAP has the func-

tionality to configure the investment groups as well as different providers with it.

Testing the Configuration

We need to do some quick checks on our savings plan configuration too. Use Transaction PA30 to create savings plan infotype 0169 for testing. Please make sure that your test case employee has infotype 0171 with correct groupings and benefits area. Figure 3.33 shows that we could use the dropdown list and select the plan that we configured. The plan has also pulled the correct employee and employer contribution variants with it. Figure 3.34 shows the contribution tab for infotype 0169. The 10% contribution in this test case helps test the percentage or dollar configuration for the employee contribution.

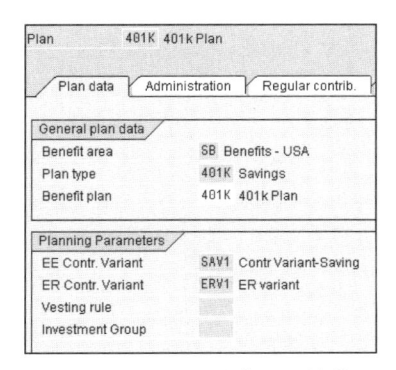

Figure 3.33 Creating Infotype 0167

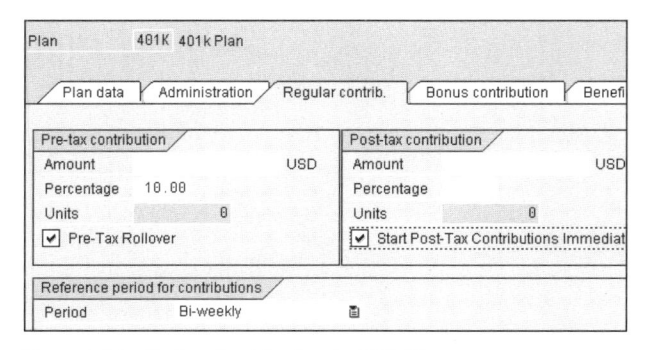

Figure 3.34 Testing Contribution to 401k Plan

3.5 Flexible Spending Account (FSA) Plans

Flexible Spending Account (FSA) plans allow participating employees to put aside pre-tax money for qualified healthcare and dependent-care expenses. Subsequently, the employee needs to complete the claims form to get qualified expenses reimbursed. As an example, suppose the co-pay for a doctor visit is $20. If the employee pays out of pocket, the cost will be $20. If the employee pays it using a FSA health-care plan, it will wind up costing less — let us say $17 — because of dollars saved by setting money aside pre-tax. Keep in mind though that not every employer offers the FSA plans.

Plan General Data

You will generally configure two plans: healthcare and dependent care. Figure 3.35 shows the simple and straightforward configuration for the healthcare account. Follow IMG menu path **Benefits • Plans • Flexible Spending Accounts Plans • Define Spending Account General Data**.

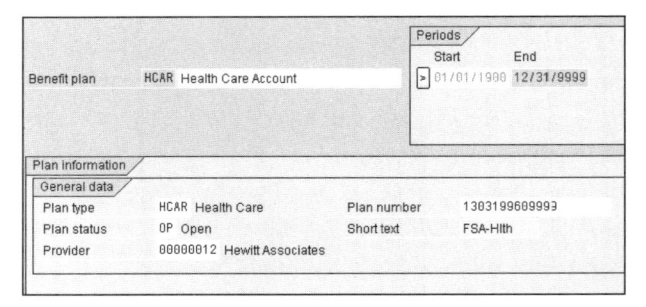

Figure 3.35 FSA Healthcare Account Plan Creation

Based on company policies and federal regulations, the maximum contribution amounts vary. In the next step of configuring attributes, we will set these amounts for the plan, Companies often outsource the FSA processing to third-party providers. In those circumstances, you will either never have to configure FSAs or you will just have to perform deduction processing in SAP. For example, an interface might send the deduction amounts from payroll to a third-party provider and subsequent claims are processed by the third-party provider.

Spending Account Attributes

Figure 3.36 shows the spending account attributes that are accessed via IMG menu path **Benefits • Plans • Flexible Spending Accounts Plans • Assign Spending Account Attribute**.

If you are managing the FSA claims processing in SAP then you will need a wage type as shown in Figure 3.36. The example in Figure 3.36 uses a **Reimburs. wage type 2X40**. Typically the previous year claims can be submitted up to March 31st of the following year. Therefore, FSA balances for two years can run in parallel in the first quarter of the calendar year.

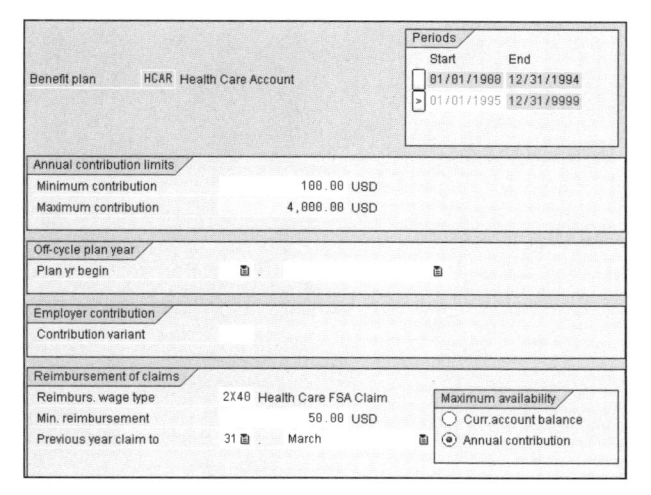

Figure 3.36 Spending Account Attributes

Defining Claim Types

Use this configuration if you are processing claims within SAP. Companies frequently outsource the FSA claims-processing work, and you may not need this configuration. The claim types are based on qualified healthcare and dependent-care expenses as defined by IRS regulations. Figure 3.37 shows a sample of claim types used in infotype 0172 for claims processing. The claim types are configured using IMG menu path **Benefits • Plans • Flexible Spending Accounts Plans • Define Spending Account Claim Types**.

Figure 3.37 Designating FSA Claim Types

Testing the Configuration

In the same way we tested in health, insurance, and savings plan, we can carry out a simple test to check the configuration. We will use Transaction PA30 and infotypes 0170 and 0172 respectively to test the FSA plans and claims. As a reminder, the infotype 171 needs to have the correct benefit area and grouping. Figure 3.38 shows the creation of an FSA plan for healthcare. Figure 3.39 presents the employee contribution tab showing the annual target amount that the employee wants to set aside pre-tax. Depending on the payroll area and frequency, periodic deductions will be made in payroll. In this example, if the employee is paid monthly then the monthly pre-tax deduction will be $2,500 divided over 12 periods.

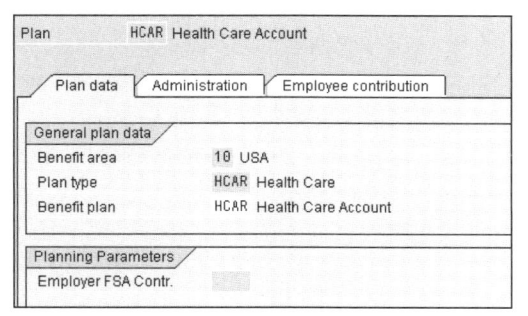

Figure 3.38 Creating FSA Plan in Infotype 0170

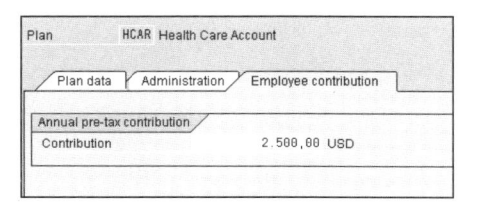

Figure 3.39 Contribution Amount in FSA Plan

Along the same line, by using Transaction PA30, we will create infotype 0172 and check whether all configuration is visible and working properly. Figure 3.40 shows the different claim types we configured earlier.

Figure 3.40 Creating Claims in Infotype 0172

3 Plan Configuration

3.6 Miscellaneous Plans

The functionality for managing miscellaneous plans helps you to build all plans that cannot be categorized under health, insurance, savings, or FSA. Therefore, the configuration is a combination of the configuration for health, insurance, and savings plans. Figure 3.41 shows the IMG content for these plans. SAP has extended the configuration from health, insurance, and savings plans all in one place to address any unique situations that you may face with non-standard benefit plans.

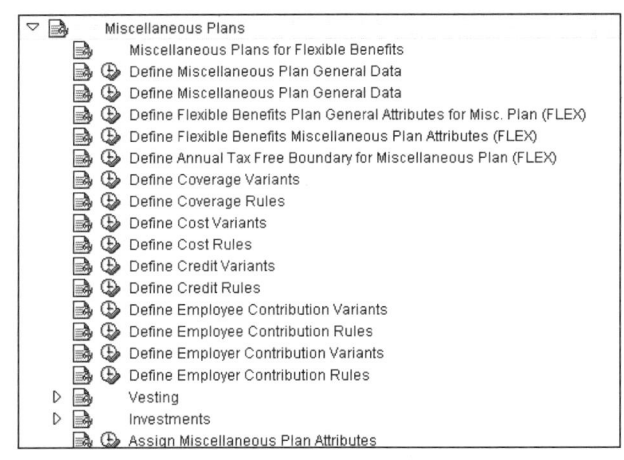

Figure 3.41 Miscellaneous Plan Configuration

Example

A company offers a plan to its senior managers whereby membership in a golf club is subsidized by the company.

Plan General Data

Figure 3.42 shows the plan **GOLF**. Note the section of screen titled **Miscellaneous plan attributes**. It shows that you can have **Cost Variants**, **Coverage Variants**, or **Contribution Variants** depending upon the nature of the plan. We have selected cost variant because this plan has costs for employee and employer. In the following sub-sections, we will use this example to configure the cost variants and rules. If you get into a situation where the miscellaneous plan requires contribution variants, then you will need to follow contribution-variant nodes in the IMG.

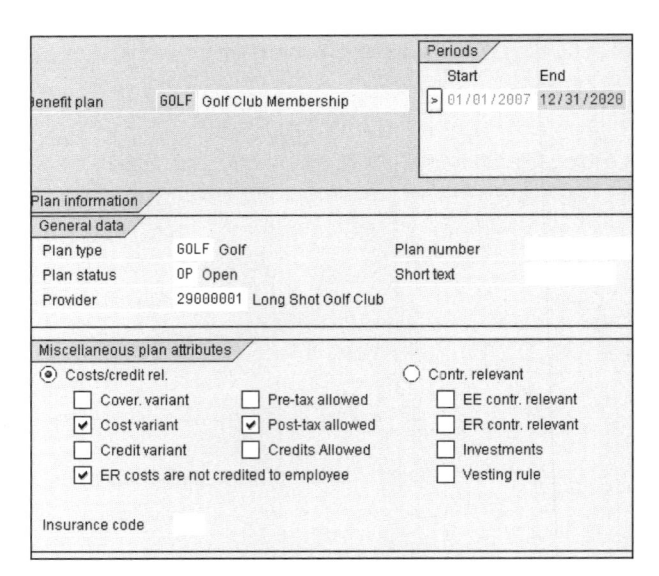

Figure 3.42 Miscellaneous Plan General Data

Defining Cost Variants and Rules

The steps that we will take here are very similar to those for health plans. We will define a cost variant and then attach a rule to the variant.

Define Cost Variant
IMG menu path **Benefits • Plans • Miscellaneous Plans • Define Cost Variants** leads us to the cost-variant example shown in Figure 3.43.

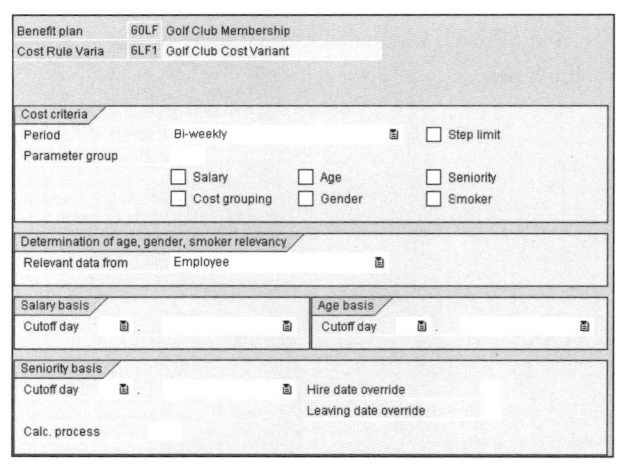

Figure 3.43 Define Cost Variant

Define Cost Rule
Following the IMG menu path **Benefits • Plans • Miscellaneous Plans • Define Cost Rules** helps us to create a cost rule for the cost variant **GLF1**. This step is, once again,

exactly the same as for the health plans described in subsection Define Cost Rules. Figure 3.44 shows the cost rule where the employee is paying $100 and the employer is paying $350 for a total cost of $450 toward the golf plan.

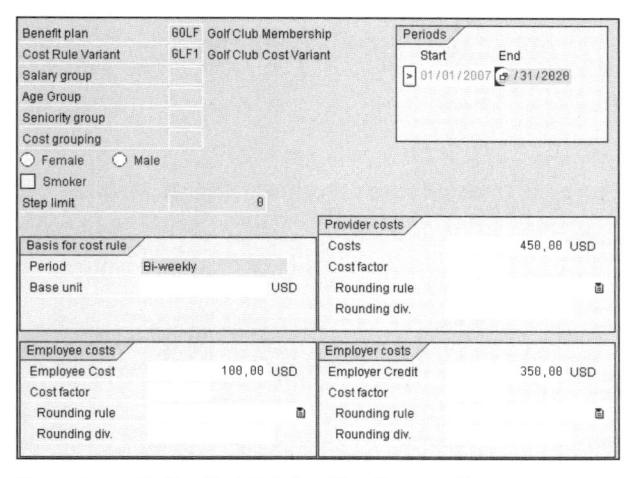

Figure 3.44 Define Cost Rule for Miscellaneous Plan

Manage Plan Attributes

Because this golf plan does not require any other configuration such as contribution or vesting rules, we can go straight to creating attributes. The IMG menu path **Benefits • Plans • Miscellaneous Plans • Assign Miscellaneous Plan Attributes** helps you to attach the cost variant to the plan. Figure 3.45 shows that we have a dummy option **OPT1** to attach the cost variant **GLF1**. In the next sub-section, when we test this configuration, you will find out that we need at least one option for the plan.

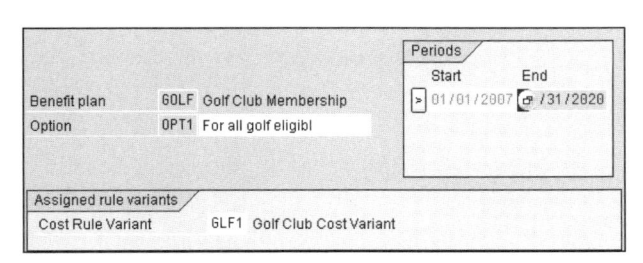

Figure 3.45 Assign Attributes for Miscellaneous Plan

Testing the Configuration

Once again, we use Transaction PA30 and the appropriate Infotype to check configuration readiness. A miscellaneous plan **GOLF** is created as shown in Figure 3.46. Figure 3.46 shows the creation of plan using infotype 0377 (miscellaneous plans). Figure 3.47 shows the cost tab for infotype 0377 and helps us make sure that the $100 employee cost and $350 employer costs are indeed flowing to the infotype.

Figure 3.46 Testing Infotype 0377 for Miscellaneous Plan

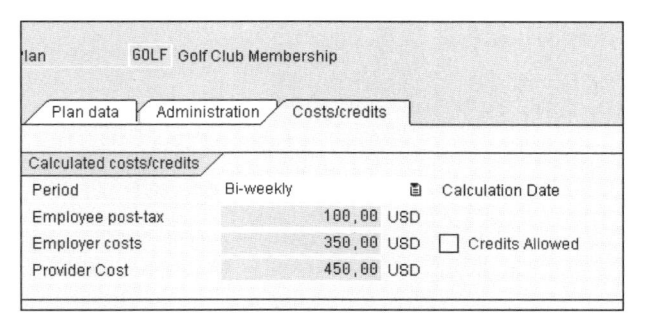

Figure 3.47 Testing Costs for Miscellaneous Plan in Infotype 0377

Now that we have configured the various plans, we need to look at what happens at Termination.

3.7 COBRA

As discussed in Chapter 1, the Consolidated Omnibus Budget Reconciliation Act (COBRA) provides continuation of health coverage at group rates to terminated employees, spouses, former spouses, and dependent children. This is available only when coverage is lost because of specific events. Just as we saw in respect to benefit changes for work and life events, COBRA has qualifying events for eligibility. There are three aspects to COBRA configuration: events, beneficiaries, and coverage. Now that we have configured the various plans, we need to look at what happens at Termination.

Defining Relevance for COBRA

The first step that we need to complete in SAP is to configure the relevance of plans (i.e., check which plans are COBRA relevant). If you follow the IMG menu path **Benefits • COBRA • Choose COBRA Plans,** you will get to the configuration shown in Figure 3.48. The plans that are available for coverage continuation are check marked. Therefore, if the employee was enrolled earlier in a plan that is not available for COBRA, after termination or qualifying COBRA event the employee will need to choose from one of the available plans for COBRA. Figure 3.48 shows that some HMO and dental plans are available, but that a medical plan is not available.

Plan	Text	Start Date	End Date	Relevant for COBRA
DENT	Company Dental Plan	01/01/1900	12/31/9999	✓
HM09	HMO Plan	01/01/2007	12/31/2010	✓
MED1	Standard Medical Plan	01/01/1990	12/31/9999	
MED2	HMO	01/01/1990	12/31/9999	✓

Figure 3.48 COBRA Relevance for Health Plans

Qualifying Events Management

As you learned at the beginning of this chapter, the qualifying events need to be managed for COBRA. Before we go to the next configuration step, we need to understand the COBRA regulation regarding continuation of coverage and the required period of coverage. For the qualifying events — and depending on whether the coverage is for a disabled person — the continuation coverage period offered varies. Figure 3.49 shows the examples of 18 months of normal coverage and 11 months of extended coverage for disabled persons in a typical termination action.

Type	Event type	Start Date	End Date	Reg. Per.	Ext.period
01	Termination of employment	04/07/1986	12/31/9999	18	11
02	Reduction in working hours	04/07/1986	12/31/9999	18	11
03	Death of employee	04/07/1986	12/31/9999	36	
04	Entitlement to Medicare	04/07/1986	12/31/9999	36	
05	Divorce	04/07/1986	12/31/9999	36	
06	Legal separation	04/07/1986	12/31/9999	36	
07	Loss of dependent status	04/07/1986	12/31/9999	36	
08	Bankruptcy of employer	04/07/1986	12/31/9999		

Figure 3.49 Qualifying Events and Coverage Continuation Period

Assign COBRA Events to Personnel Actions

The qualifying events for COBRA are typically driven from PA actions. Therefore, PA actions with their reason codes need to be linked to COBRA events. The IMG menu path **Benefits • COBRA • Assign COBRA Events to Personnel Actions** allows you to do that. Figure 3.50 shows samples of IPA actions linked with COBRA events.

Act.	Name of action type	ActR	Event type	Text
10	Termination	01	01	Termination of employment
10	Termination	02	01	Termination of employment
10	Termination	03	01	Termination of employment
10	Termination	09	03	Death of employee
10	Termination	20	01	Termination of employment
10	Termination	E1	01	Termination of employment

Figure 3.50 Linking PA Actions to COBRA Events

Define Processing Parameters for Benefits Area

In Chapter 2, we saw that the benefits area has administrative parameters. Similarly, the benefits area has parameters for COBRA. Using IMG menu path **Benefits • COBRA • Define Processing Parameters,** you can set the parameters. You will notice in Figure 3.51 that the parameters will also have an impact on our earlier step concerning which COBRA events to use for linking PA actions.

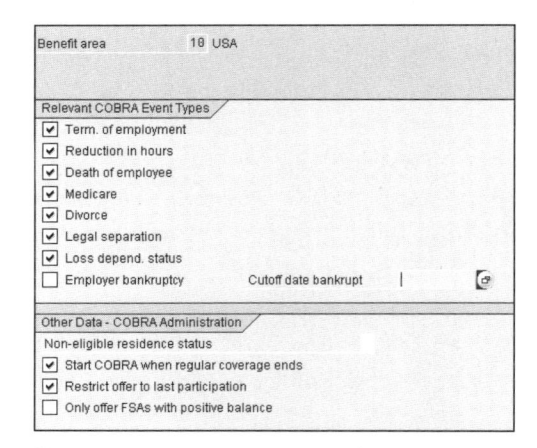

```
Benefit area            10 USA

Relevant COBRA Event Types
  ☑ Term. of employment
  ☑ Reduction in hours
  ☑ Death of employee
  ☑ Medicare
  ☑ Divorce
  ☑ Legal separation
  ☑ Loss depend. status
  ☐ Employer bankruptcy    Cutoff date bankrupt

Other Data - COBRA Administration
  Non-eligible residence status
  ☑ Start COBRA when regular coverage ends
  ☑ Restrict offer to last participation
  ☐ Only offer FSAs with positive balance
```

Figure 3.51 Processing Parameters for COBRA Events

In the Chapter 4, you will learn how to use the COBRA functionality available in SAP to use this configuration.

3.8 Summary

The configuration of a benefit plan is repetitive in nature. Once you complete the steps for one type of benefit plan, you can do it for the others much faster. SAP follows a design approach that is based on variants and rules. Hopefully, this chapter has helped you understand the underlying concept.

Parameter groupings and driving employee costs based on certain groupings can be a little confusing when you work with them for the first time, but after you understand the concept for one type of plan you can repeat the magic for other plan types. In Chapter 4, we will apply this knowledge and get to the application side of the product to learn the administration of benefits.

4 Managing Benefits Administration

In this chapter we will discuss how to manage the benefit changes due to employee life events. This functionality will work well in the SAP application worked on so far, as long as your configuration from earlier chapters is in alignment.

In the discussion of benefit plans in Chapter 3 we used a short-cut to check the readiness of our configuration. We primarily used Transaction PA30 for infotype maintenance to check the plan configuration. However, in reality, benefits enrollment is handled through the Enrollment Monitor as well as Employee Self Service (ESS) tools. In Chapter 2 (Section 2.7), you learned about the benefits-adjustment reasons and how these reasons are linked with the benefit plan changes. In this chapter, you will learn about the Enrollment Monitor, and, hopefully, the configuration between adjustment reasons and benefit plans will start making sense.

Let us start the discussion with the Enrollment Monitor and sample enrollment scenarios. We will use the schematic in Figure 4.1 to represent the discussion in this Chapter. It shows the employee benefits life cycle and the impact on benefits.

The events are as follows:

- Employee joins the organization and gets to elect benefits
- Employee may have work and life events that require the employee to change or add benefit plans or change dependents and/or beneficiaries
- During annual enrollment, the employee again has a chance to change and re-elect the benefits
- If the employee resigns or leaves for other reasons, then benefits are terminated and de-limited.

This simple life cycle illustrates the benefits of administration and the impact of the earlier configuration.

4.1 Enrollment Monitor

Before we move to the Enrollment Monitor, let us revisit the administrative parameters for our benefits area. Figure 4.2 shows the open-enrollment dates for the benefits area, which we will use later in this discussion.

Example

Because the employee is joining in July, he gets to elect the benefits in July and then has a second chance to change them during open enrollment when it starts on November 1st.

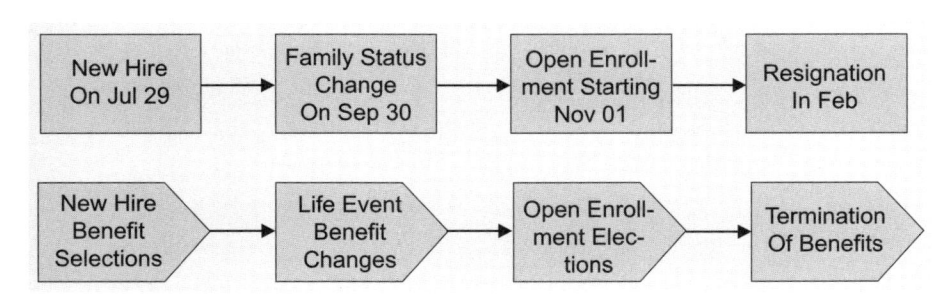

Figure 4.1 Benefits Administration Life Cycle

4 Managing Benefits Administration

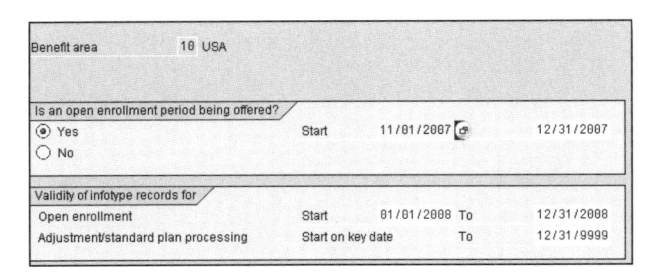

Figure 4.2 Open Enrollment Dates for Benefits Area

The discussion starts with the use of the Benefits Enrollment Monitor. On the application side, if you follow the menu path **Personnel Management • Benefits • Enrollment,** you will get to the Enrollment Monitor.

New Hire Elections/Enrollment

For the new employee, infotype 0171 and infotype 0378 are prerequisites. Figure 4.3 shows infotype 0378 with **New Hire Event** as the **Adjustment Reason**.

> **Tip**
>
> You can refer to Chapter 2 to review the adjustment reasons and their impact on benefit plans.

Figure 4.3 Benefits Adjustment Reason

The **Adjustment Reason** in Figure 4.3 is the result of the configuration shown in Figure 4.4. Figure 4.4 has configuration for **Adjustment Reason HIRE**. This configuration tells us that if the employee joined on 7/29/2007, he has two months to decide on elections. Figure 4.3 has infotype 0378 showing the two-month period.

Now, the employee, through ESS or the HR manager using the employee's paper-based election forms, goes to the Enrollment Monitor. The Enrollment Monitor shown in Figure 4.5 displays the **New Hire Event** with the two-month period for election.

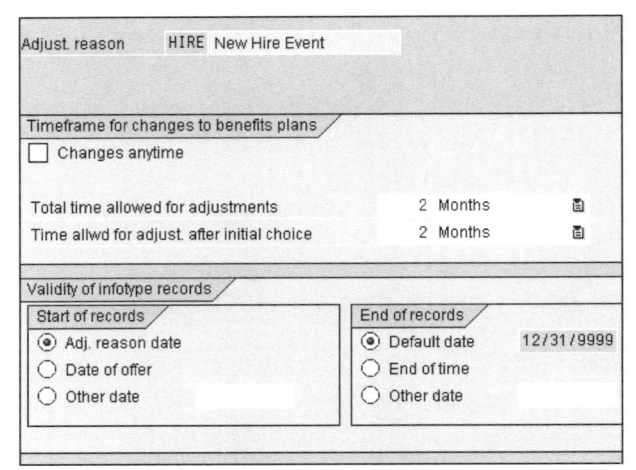

Figure 4.4 Adjustment Reason Configuration

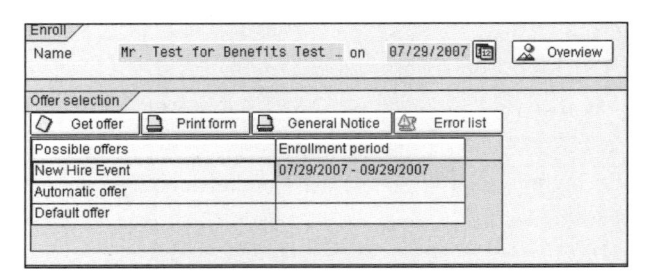

Figure 4.5 New Hire Event in the Enrollment Monitor

When you click on the **New-Hire Event** (in Figure 4.5), you will see the plans this employee is eligible for, based on the Adjustment Reason, the infotype 0171 groupings, and the related programs' configuration.

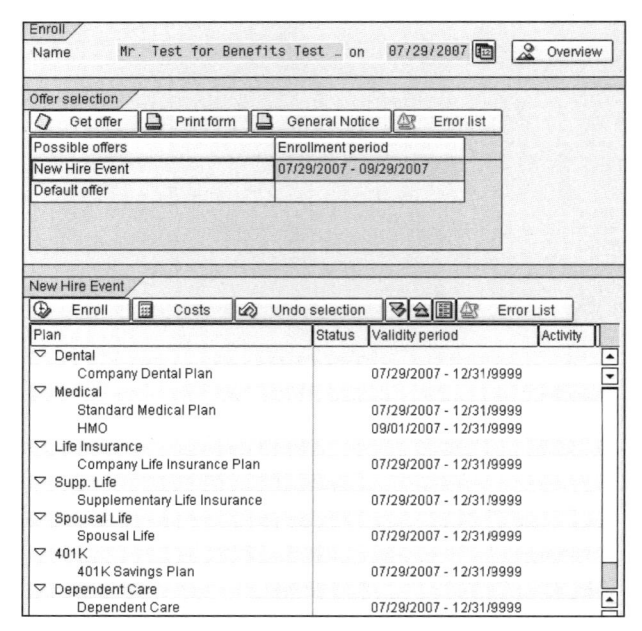

Figure 4.6 Eligible Plans for New Hire Event

Employees then select the plans as shown in Figure 4.7. The overlapping screen shows the **Accept** button the employees use when they make their selections.

Finally, when the employee completes his election, all benefit infotypes (0167, 0168, 0169, 0170) are created in the background in the employee's master data (see Figure 4.8).

The new employee is now enrolled in the plans he selected. The next events to consider are possible life changes.

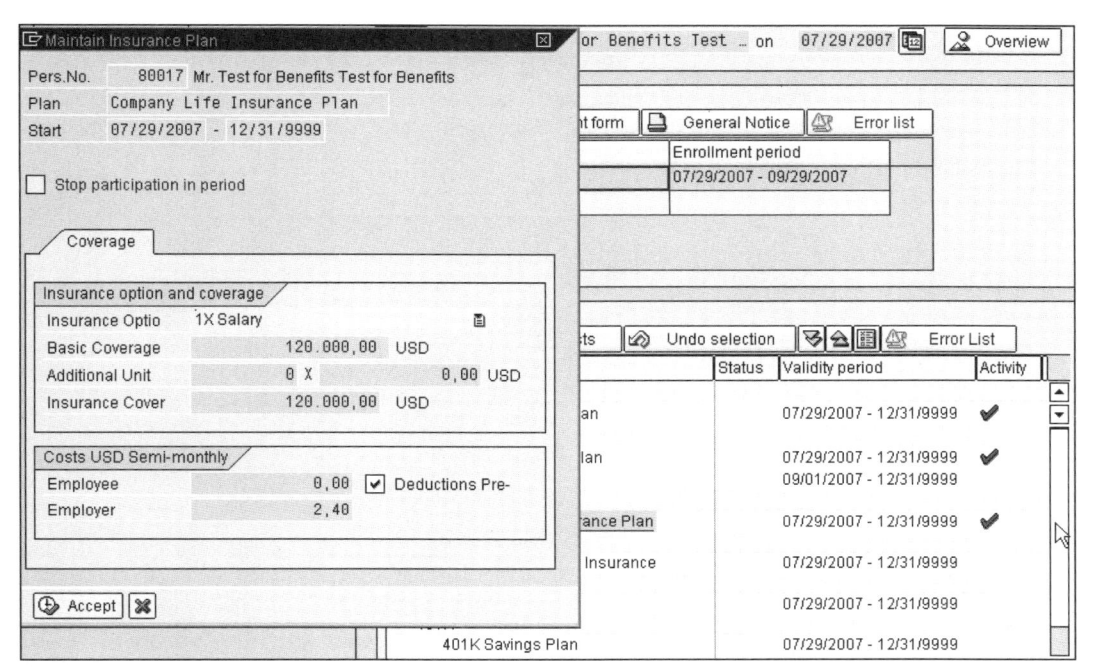

Figure 4.7 Choosing the Plan

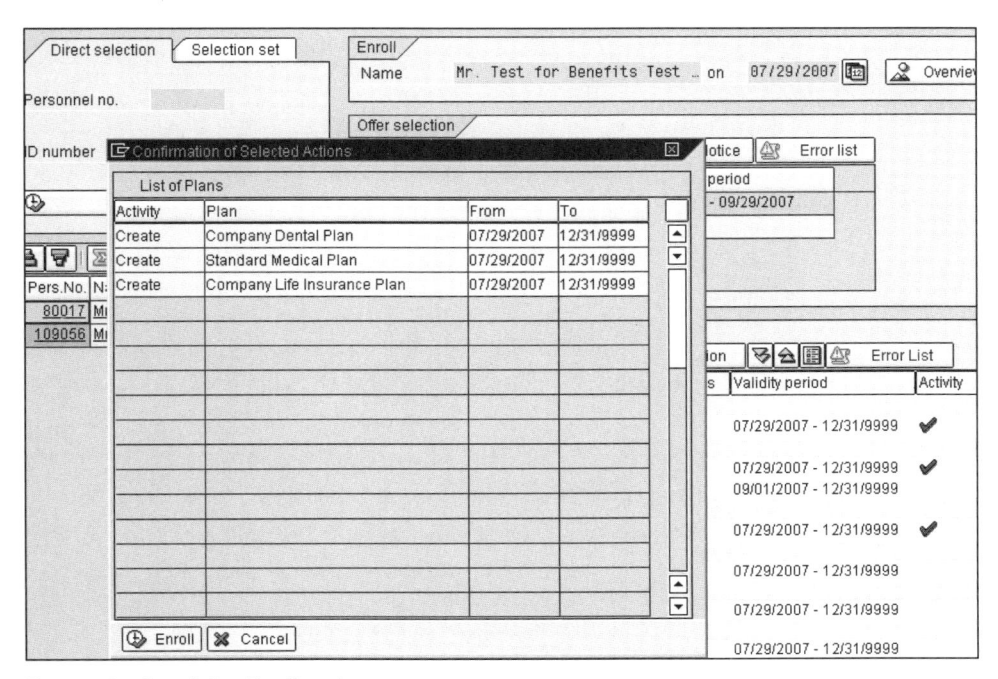

Figure 4.8 Completing Enrollment

Employee Life Event Changes

Following our schematic flow shown in Figure 4.1, let us say that the employee has a family status change a few months after joining. In September, the employee had a new baby — definitely an important life event. Figure 4.9 shows the infotype 0378 for the same employee after the life event was managed, which is usually done through a Personnel Action. Some implementations use Transaction PA30 (maintenance of employee data) to maintain the Infotypes instead of actions. In addition, benefits administration users also like the Transaction HRBEN0001 (also known as Benefits Monitor) for enrolling employees into benefit plans.

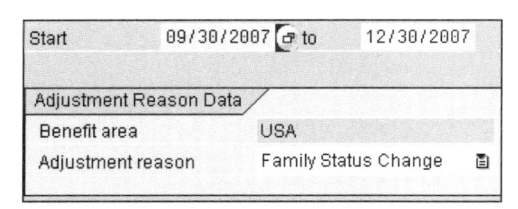

Figure 4.9 Employee Life Event Infotype 0378

If you recall, the work we did in Chapter 2, makes this change possible because of our permissibility configuration. Figure 4.10 shows the Adjustment Reason and the associated health plans that the employee is allowed to change.

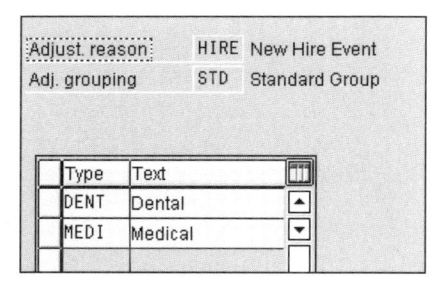

Figure 4.10 Permissibility of Health Plans for Reason

Once again, the employee can go to ESS and access the Benefits enrollment (similar to benefits monitor from backend SAP) as shown in Figure 4.11, or can go to the HR representative and perform the change on paper. The example in Figure 4.11 shows the life event and a three-month period allowed for election. Typically, this will be a 30-day period that most organizations allow their employees for any changes caused by life events.

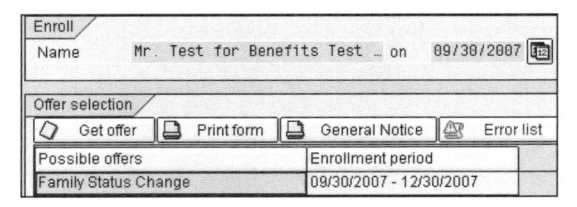

Figure 4.11 Life Event Election Change

When you click on the highlighted line, the benefit plans that are allowed are listed, as shown in Figure 4.12.

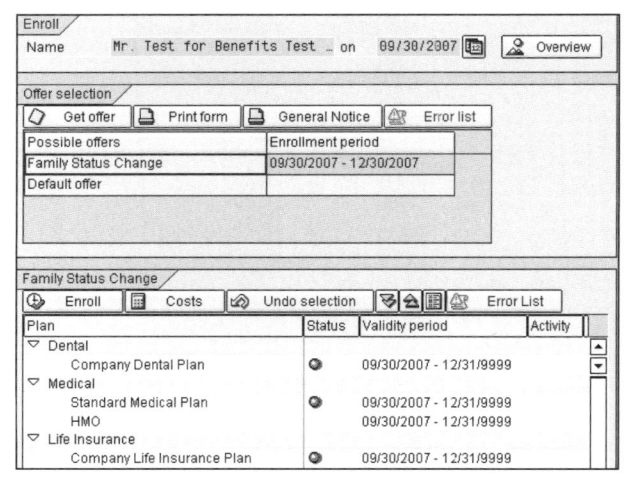

Figure 4.12 Plan Changes for Life Event

The bullets under **Status** show that the employee is now enrolled in those plans and can go into the system and change the options for dependent coverage, etc.

> **Tip**
>
> When you test this functionality in the SAP system, you will find that the system follows color coding: a green bullet if the enrollment is error free and a red bullet if there is any error or problem.

Note that the **Validity period** is starting on the **Family Status Change** date, because this event was configured to allow changes. The **Family Status Change** line that you see in Figure 4.12 is based on infotype 0378 for this employee, with the appropriate adjustment-reason code configuration. This same process will apply to all work and life events that have been configured to permit changes to benefit elections.

Open Enrollment Elections

Now let us fast forward our employee from September to November. Starting November 1st, the company offers the open-enrollment period. Figure 4.13 shows the Benefits Monitor with the **Open offer** line and its associated plans.

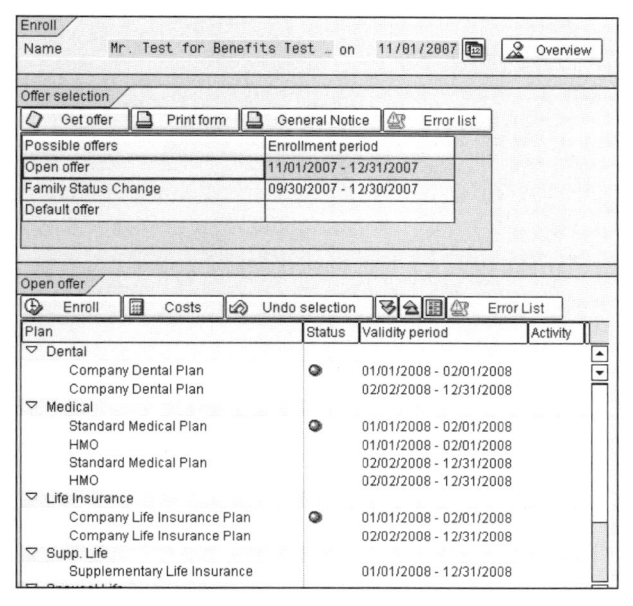

Figure 4.13 Open Enrollment

Once again, the employee follows a process similar to the one used during **New Hire** enrollment. However, in the new year's enrollment, the company may offer different plans, so the employee will get the chance to elect new, better options. Alternatively, employees can decide to continue with existing plans, but normally this still requires action on the employee's part.

Now that you know about the process for enrollment and election changes, let us see the impact of an employee resignation or termination.

4.2 Termination Monitor

To get started with our discussion of the Termination Monitor, please refer back to the schematic in Figure 4.1. And once again, we fast forward the employee's life cycle to February of the following year (2008). At this point, the employee decides to leave the organization and submits his resignation. Through a Personnel Action, the HR department will terminate the employee and change his status as of his last day of employment (in the U.S., two weeks' notice is typically a convention when an employee resigns).

Tip

If you don't remember the termination reasons and groupings, you can refer back to Section 2.6 of Chapter 2.

Access the Termination Monitor using the menu path **Personnel Management • Benefits • Termination** as illustrated in Figure 4.14. The termination date is 2/1/2008 for this employee, as shown in the last column titled **Date** in Figure 4.14.

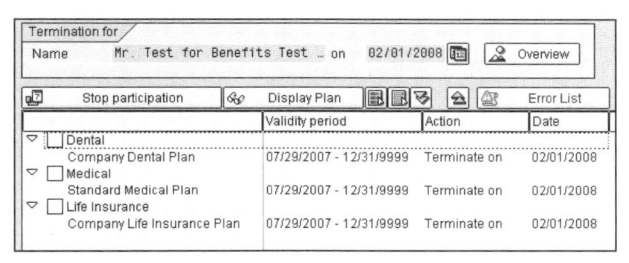

Figure 4.14 Termination Monitor

The HR department user who is running the termination will typically select all of the plans as shown in Figure 4.15 and de-limit the plans and participation.

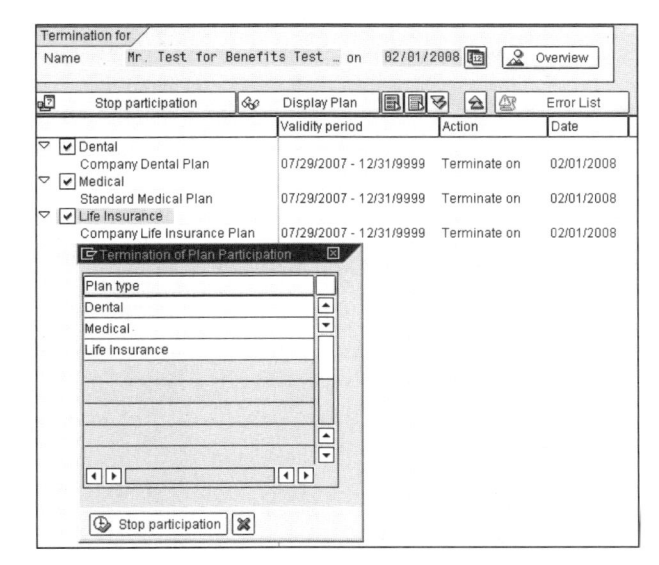

Figure 4.15 Terminating Plans

4 Managing Benefits Administration

After you click on the **Stop-participation** button (Figure 4.15, lower left), SAP will show a confirmation message as seen in Figure 4.16.

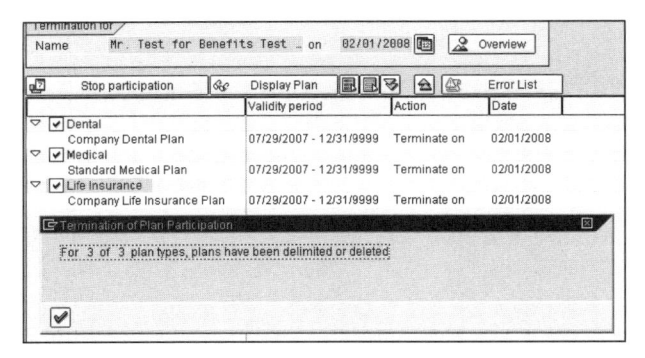

Figure 4.16 Completing Plans De-Limiting

Subsequently, if you check the employee's data using Transaction PA30, you will find that the appropriate benefits infotypes are de-limited.

Immediately after the employee leaves, he is asked whether he wants to take advantage of the COBRA option. At this point, the benefits administration enters the new phase of COBRA administration.

> **Note**
> Participants and beneficiaries should receive the COBRA communication no later than 14 days after the plan administrator receives notice of a qualifying COBRA event.

4.3 Managing COBRA

In our earlier example, the employee has left, and therefore the COBRA process should start covering the employee. The process starts with Event Collection.

1. The Events-collection menu path **Personnel Management • Benefits • COBRA • Event Collection** helps us create the COBRA options based on the reason configurations we learned in Chapter 2.

   Figure 4.17 shows the Event Collection output. You will notice that the terminated employee from our example appears in the output.

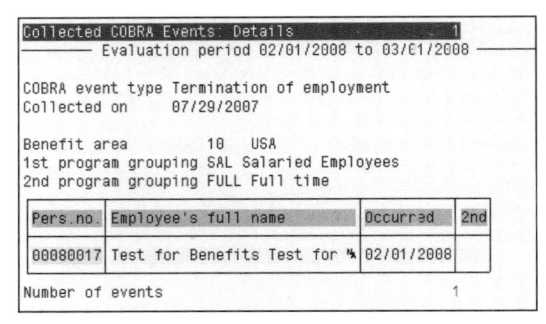

Figure 4.17 COBRA Events Collection

2. Letter Generation is the next step. After the COBRA events are collected, you can generate standard letters using the menu path **Personnel Management • Benefits • COBRA • Letter Generation**. Figure 4.18 shows the screen where you can select the employees for Letter Generation.

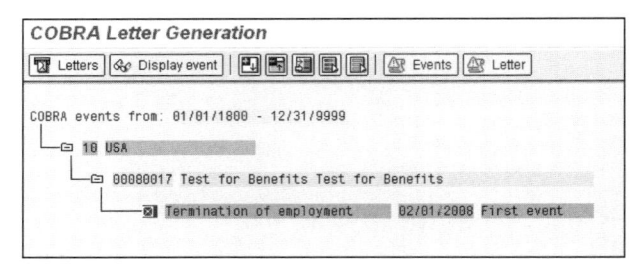

Figure 4.18 Letter Generation

At this stage, the employee can either choose to decline participation or elect COBRA coverage.

3. When the employee chooses to elect COBRA plans, the process is very similar to a normal enrollment. Using menu path **Personnel Management • Benefits • COBRA • Participation**, you can get to the COBRA Participation Monitor. For our test employee, Figure 4.19 shows the result.

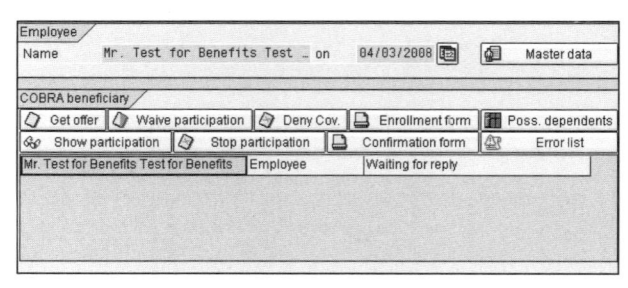

Figure 4.19 COBRA Participation Monitor

4. The COBRA enrollment process works similarly to the processes we used during our new-hire and open-

enrollment processes. Figure 4.20 shows that the two plans have been selected for participation.

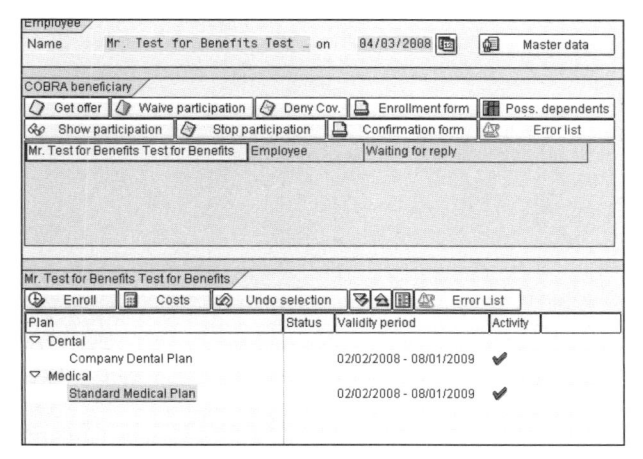

Figure 4.20 Election of COBRA Plans

Unlike a normal, active employee, an employee in the COBRA plan does not have payroll processing. Therefore, SAP has provided cost reports to allow for collection of the plan costs from the employee. Menu path **Personnel Management • Benefits • COBRA • Cost Summary** shows the cost due from the employee (Figure 4.21).

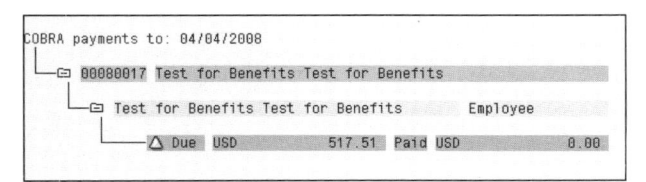

Figure 4.21 COBRA Cost Summary

SAP has also provided other useful tools in the Benefits module that are very helpful for checking your configurations and assisting with benefits administration.

4.4 Useful Tools

Let us cover a few of these tools to give you an idea of what is available.

Overview of Plans

In the IMG, you will find a great tool for getting an overview of the plan, appropriately called the Plan Overview. While you are testing, you can access the IMG menu **Benefits • Toolset • Plan Overview,** and you will be able to run the Plan Overview tool for specific benefits areas. Figure 4.22 shows the output. You can explode the report to see the details on eligibility rules and termination rules, and you can access the features.

Plan Cost Summary

Another useful tool is the Plan Cost Summary, which allows you to run a useful report showing a cost summary. You can access this tool via the IMG menu **Benefits • Toolset • Plan Cost Summary.** This report is quite useful after completing the configuration, when you can ensure that all the costs are configured correctly. Figure 4.23 presents the sample of this report.

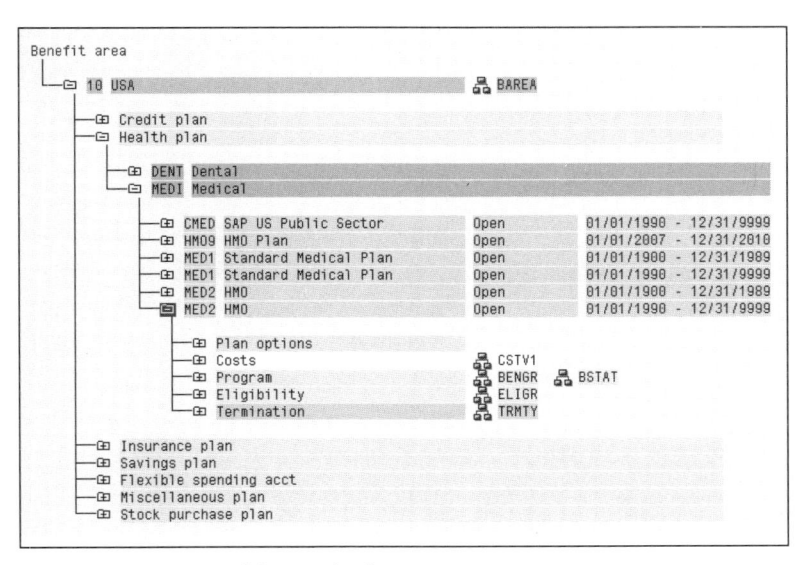

Figure 4.22 Overview of the Benefit Plans

4 Managing Benefits Administration

Figure 4.23 Plan Cost Summary

Configuration Consistency Check

The configuration of the Benefits module, as you have seen so far in this book, can get confusing because of all the variants, rules, and groupings. SAP has provided another very useful tool to check the consistency of your configurations and to make the testing process much easier. In the IMG, follow the menu path **Benefits • Toolset • Configuration Consistency Check** to access this tool, as seen in Figure 4.24.

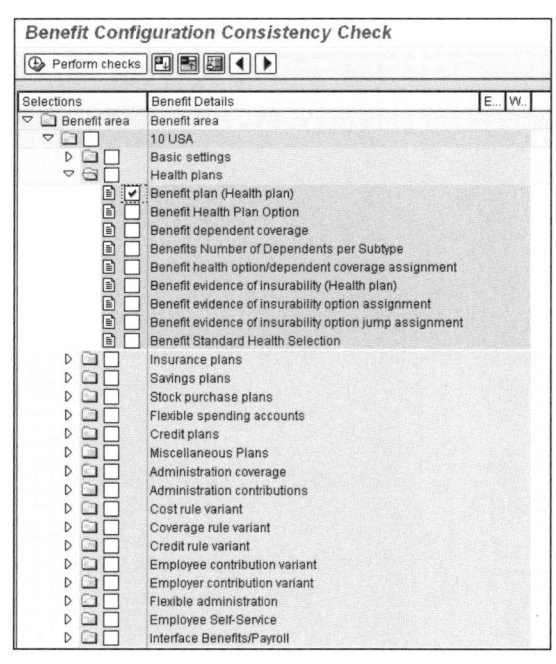

Figure 4.24 Configuration Consistency Check

You should also note that the Configuration Consistency Check can be carried out in almost all areas by clicking the check box. Subsequently clicking on the performance check button in the screen gives you the results as seen in Figure 4.25. Note that this sample configuration has error messages and warnings that need to be explored further.

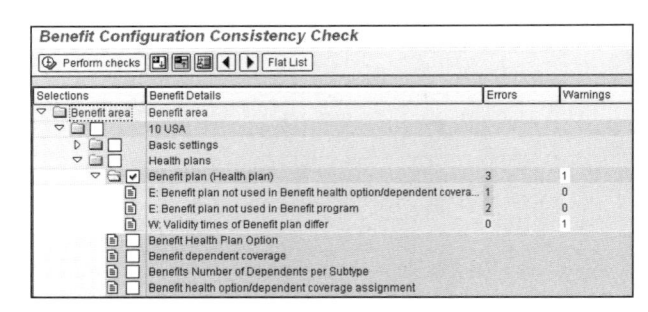

Figure 4.25 Results of Consistency Check

Overview of Adjustment Permissions

After completing the configuration, you should always confirm the adjustment reasons and associated permissions. To do this, you should allow the menu path in the IMG **Benefits • Flexible Administration • Benefit Adjustment Reasons • Define Adjustment Permissions • Overview of Adjustment Permissions**. This allows you to run the report for a Benefit Area and Plan Type combination. The sample output in Figure 4.26 is for health plans. The output shows which plans are allowed to be added, changed, or deleted based on the adjustment reason in infotype 0378.

Adj.reason	Gr...	Plan type	Change plan	Add plan	Delete plan	Chg.opt.	Chg.depcov	Chg. dep.	Chg.pretax
FAM	STD	DENT	X	X	X	X	X	X	
		MEDI	X	X	X	X	X	X	
HIRE		DENT		X		X	X	X	
		MEDI		X		X	X	X	
JOB		DENT	X	X	X	X	X	X	
		MEDI	X	X	X	X	X	X	
RET		DENT	X	X	X	X	X	X	X
		MEDI	X	X	X	X	X	X	X

Figure 4.26 Adjustment Permissions Overview

4.5 Summary

The configuration performed in the IMG is the foundation and building blocks on which benefits administration is based. It also helps you better understand the configuration you did in earlier plans and in the flexible administration portion of the IMG. Throughout this book, we have been discussing the employee life cycle. If you continue to take this approach - thinking in terms of hiring, life events, and termination - it will help you to master the benefits administration life cycle from enrollment to COBRA.

In the next chapter, we will review the essential technical tools for the Benefits module.

5 Technical Support

The SAP Benefits module typically requires more technical development than other SAP HR modules, because of its focus on Employee Self Service (ESS), data transfer to benefits providers, and statutory communications. This chapter will give you an overview of the available technical tools that address these requirements.

The Benefits module in SAP requires technical development support, particularly as related to Employee Self Service (ESS), forms, user exits, and interfaces. These areas always top the list when it comes to the implementation of the Benefits module. Unfortunately, implementation teams often underestimate the efforts and skills required in the technical areas, so the purpose of this chapter is to familiarize functional configuration team members with the various technical support tools and the skills required to use them. The chapter does not go into technical customizing details.

We will begin the discussion with *Forms*.

5.1 Forms

The forms normally used in the Benefits processes include:

- Benefits Enrollment Confirmation, Changes to Plans Confirmation, Confirmation of life events
- General notices
- COBRA letter
- 401k Contribution Change Confirmation
- HIPAA forms
- Total Compensation Statement

In the IMG, if you follow a menu path **Benefits · Flex Admin · Form Set Up · Set up SAPscript template**, you will reach the forms tree as shown in Figure 5.1. When you select a form from the SAP-displayed tree, SAP starts the form editor Transaction SE71 to allow you to edit the forms as shown in Figure 5.2. This is a traditional SAPscript form editor. However, SAP now offers you three choices related to forms:

1. Traditional SAPscript forms as shown in Figure 5.1 and 5.2
2. Adobe forms
3. Office templates to print from your PC's default printer

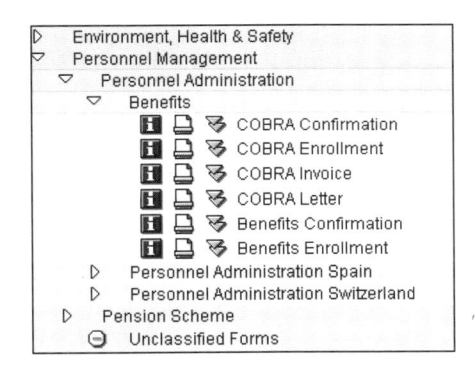

Figure 5.1 Accessing the SAPscript Form

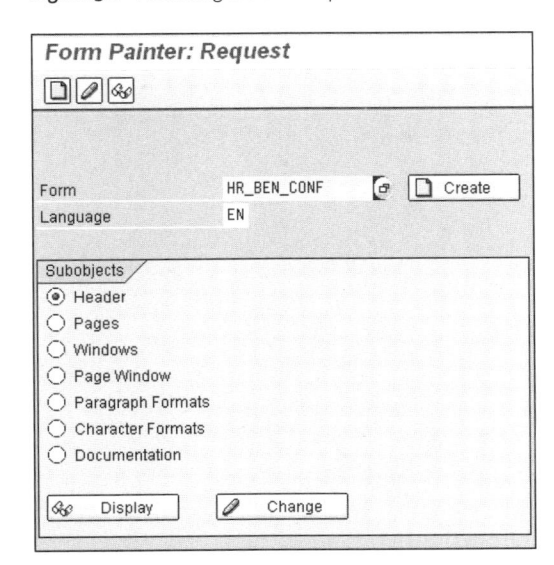

Figure 5.2 Forms Editor — Transaction SE71

5 Technical Support

When you use the IMG path **Benefits • Flex Admin • Form Set up • Assign Form Type** you can link the Adobe forms to the **Benefits Enrollment**. Figure 5.3 shows the sample screen. (You will need the required Adobe toolset to develop the Adobe forms.) Typically, every implementation team needs to customize the forms to suit their requirements, including an individual company logo. Example: Enrollment confirmation form or Confirmation of benefits changes.

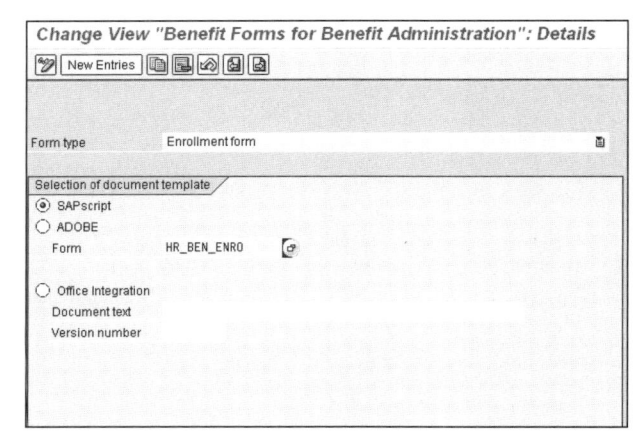

Figure 5.3 Form Type

To test the enrollment forms, you will need to use the application menu **Benefits • Forms • Enrollment**.

User Exits provide the next useful tool that we will review for Benefits technical work.

5.2 User Exits

SAP has provided the concept of User Exits in many modules, not just in the Benefits and HR modules. User Exits provide a way to call a function module.

Example

SAP provided a User Exit PBEN0008 for function HR_BEN_CALC_BENEFIT_COST.

The User Exits help customers make enhancements to functionality without modifying the SAP system, so it is always helpful to search for User Exits. To better understand the User Exits, try to search for PBEN0008.

1. Searching the User Exit, you can use Transaction CMOD to look for a User Exit. From Transaction CMOD, use the menu path **Utilities • SAP Enhancements**. Figure 5.4 shows the screen that lists all available User Exits. Assuming that you don't know the names, you can just list all available User Exits.

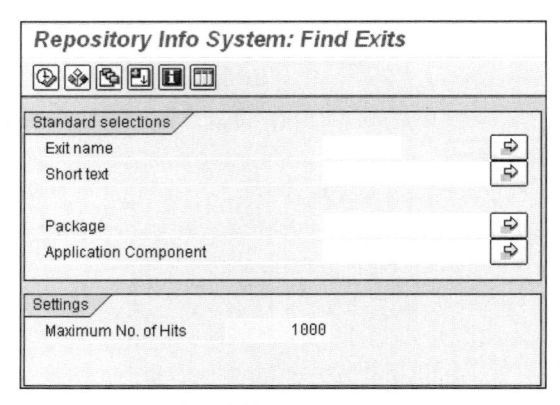

Figure 5.4 List of Available User Exits

2. Figure 5.5 shows the available benefits User Exits, so select **PBEN0008**.

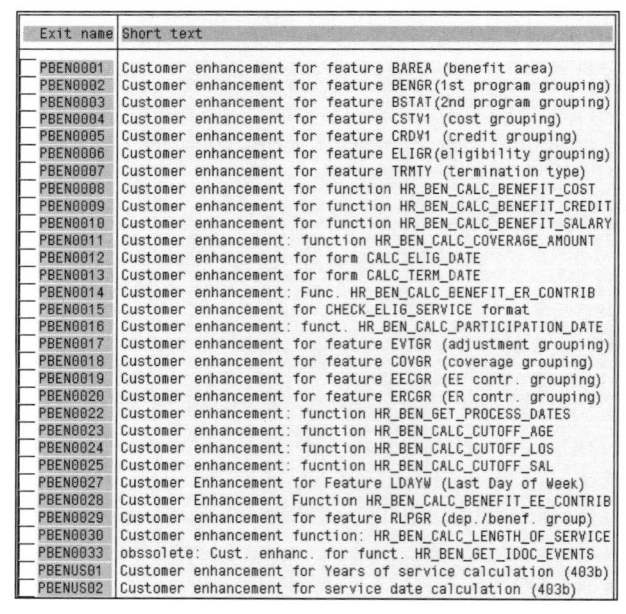

Figure 5.5 Benefits User Exits

3. Figure 5.6 shows the function-module name that can be used to make a **CALL**, as a result of User Exit **PBEN0008**.

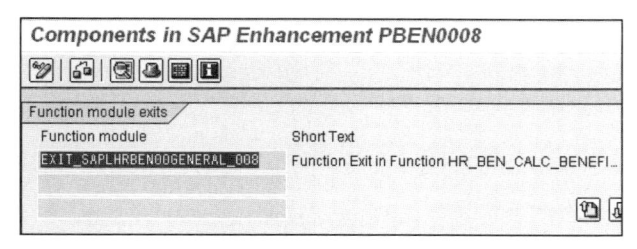

Figure 5.6 Function Module for Benefits User Exit

You will need a good ABAP programmer to help you use this functionality, if you land in situations such as:

- Overriding the costs in Benefits while maintaining infotype 0167 or 0168
- Changing eligibility rules beyond the configured eligibility rules and program groupings

In the next section, we will move on to cover Interfaces, which can often be very complex.

5.3 Interfaces

Benefits implementations are very complex because they need to communicate with the benefits providers or vendors. Earlier, in Chapter 2, you learned about creating the benefit providers in the Benefits module. The Benefits module needs to "communicate" with the benefits providers about an employee's enrollment, family details, 401k contributions, etc. This communication of data is normally done via interfaces. The interfaces send the data in particular file formats and layouts to benefits providers. The data transfer in many cases could be in both directions: inbound to SAP from some of the providers and outbound from SAP to the providers.

The following are some of the generally used sample outbound interfaces:

- Outbound employee data from SAP to benefit providers, giving details of the employee and their dependents
- Outbound election and enrollment data related to plans. (Because providers are different for different plans, you will need to design and create interfaces for each vendor.)
- Outbound 401k contribution data to savings plan vendors
- Outbound employee data for pension plans
- Outbound data from payroll for actual deductions involving employee and employer amounts
- Outbound COBRA events data in situations when COBRA is outsourced

SAP has delivered a program that you access through the applications menu path **Benefits • Administration • Data Transfer to Provider,** as shown in Figure 5.7. This program will help you run delivered IDocs for outbound interfaces.

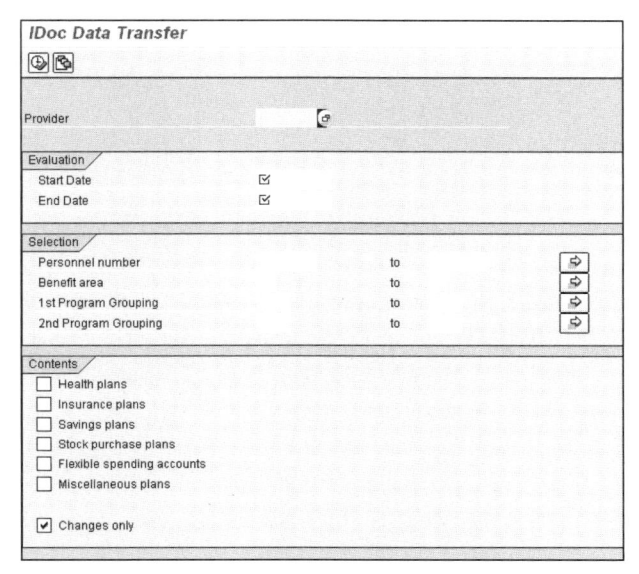

Figure 5.7 Running Outbound Interfaces

We will not discuss IDoc customizing in this book, but for those of you who are interested, you can use Transactions WE20 and WE30 to access the IDoc menu. The IDoc menu uses different partner types and the delivered partner type Benefits Provider (BP) is used to link the Benefits IDocs.

Similar to outbound interfaces, the Benefits module may have requirements for inbound interfaces. Some typical cases are listed here:

- Inbound data from flexible spending claims when the claims processing is outsourced
- Long-term disability (LTD) provider incoming data when employees directly deal with the LTD provider
- Pension plan provider incoming data

Implementation teams are sometimes divided over the use of tools in SAP. Some choose to go with traditional ABAP development, while others look at XI/XML technology. XML technology is more recent, and if you want to learn more about developments in XML, especially in the benefits field, you may want to visit HR-XML Consortium's website (*www.hr-xml.org*), which has valuable resources on this topic.

Now we will move on to Data conversion.

5.4 Data Conversion

The data conversion prior to go-live of the Benefits module depends on the timing of go-live. Many implementations choose the popular January 1st date for go-live, especially when the implementation includes payroll. Many organizations offer an open-enrollment period during November and December of the prior year; therefore, you may have to be prepared to convert the enrollment data from a legacy system to SAP when you are transitioning to SAP from a legacy system. This will involve:

- Conversion of applicable benefit infotypes (0167, 0168, 0169, and 0170, etc.)
- Mapping and conversion of infotype 0171 (program groupings) prior to converting the plan infotypes. This could be tricky due to the HR structures and the applicable impact on infotype 0171
- Balances for flexible spending accounts for the prior year, so that claims can be processed until March 31st. You will need to handle both the current-year and prior-year balances, because employees can submit claims until March 31st.
- In addition, you will need to keep an eye on work and life events during the data conversion cut-off periods. Examples include:
  - Terminations after the cut-off date for data conversion and their impact on COBRA events
  - New hires after the open-enrollment and when you have a cut-off date for data conversion such that new hire enrollments are not included in the data extractions from legacy systems
  - Additions of dependents after the cut-off date

And of course, our discussion on technical topics would not be complete without reference to Employee Self Service (ESS).

5.5 Basics of Employee Self Service (ESS)

The Benefits module is probably the one module that truly maximizes the potential of ESS functionality in SAP. SAP's ESS functionality for Benefits includes:

- Enrollment
- Participation overview
- FSA account claims

In Figure 5.8, you can see a simple out of the box portal picture showing ESS. The different tabs that you see under ESS are referred to as areas.

If you follow the menu path in the IMG **Cross-Application Components • Homepage Framework • Areas • Define Areas,** you will get to Figure 5.9. In this figure you will see the **Benefits** and **Payments** entry that is a tab as shown earlier Figure 5.8.

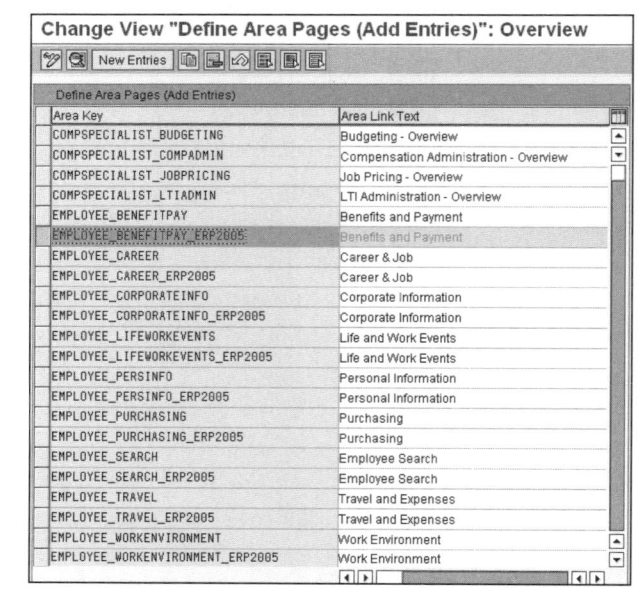

Figure 5.9 Define Areas

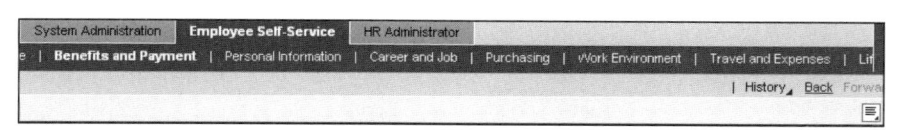

Figure 5.8 Out of the Box ESS

In each Area, you will have options for the employees as shown in Figure 5.10. When the ESS user (employee) clicks on the option, it will execute a Transaction or bring up a functionality. This is controlled by "services" in SAP.

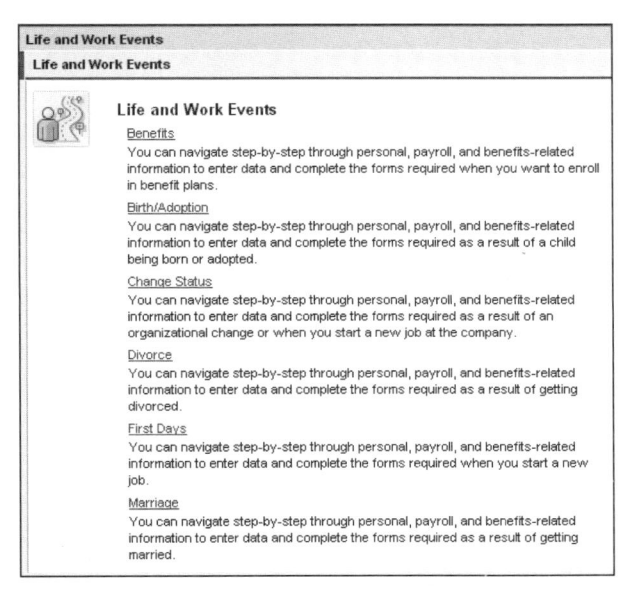

Figure 5.10 Options Under an Area

If you are interested in investigating this topic further, you can follow the IMG menu path **Cross-Application Components • Homepage Framework** to understand SAP's delivered content. In this menu, follow the sub-path **Cross-Application Components • Homepage Framework • Services • Define Services • Define Services (Add Entries)** to get to the screen shown in Figure 5.11. You will see the delivered SAP services for the Benefits module. You can copy and modify the services to customize them for your own implementation.

In the ESS portal when the employee clicks on an option as shown in Figure 5.10, there will be a Transaction. Figure 5.12 is a sample of enrollment, similar to the enrollment that we saw earlier in Chapter 4, but in this case, the employee is using ESS to carry out the same functionality.

In addition, you will also need to complete the configuration in the Benefits module. Use the IMG menu path **Benefits • Employee Self Service** to get to the configuration. For your benefits area, you need to complete the parameters using the IMG menu path **Benefits • Employee Self Service • Set ESS Parameters**. Figure 5.13 shows the parameter screen for a **Benefits area**.

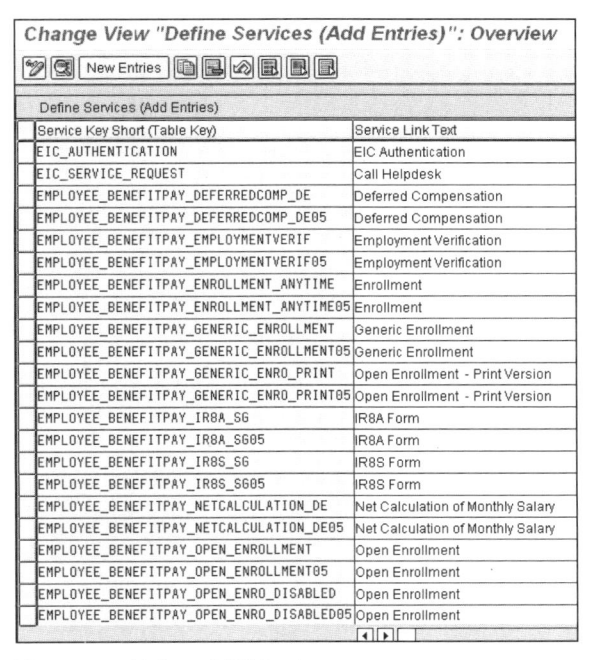

Figure 5.11 Delivered ESS Services

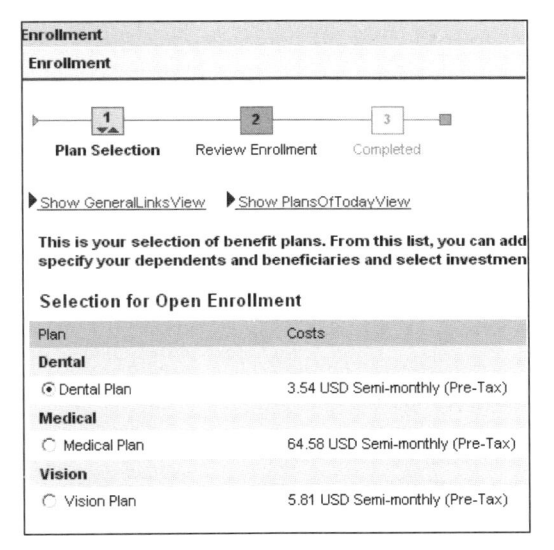

Figure 5.12 Enrollment using ESS

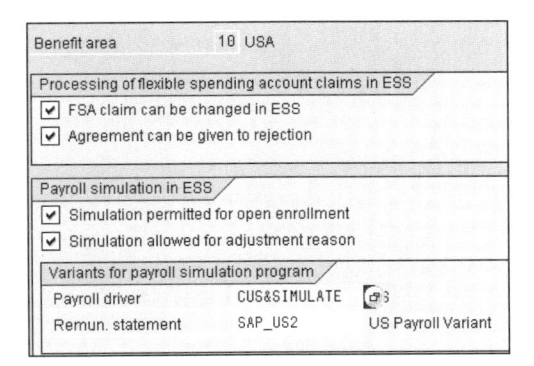

Figure 5.13 ESS Parameters for Benefits Area

In the same menu path, you will be able to link URLs for the benefit providers. The IMG path **Benefits • Employee Self Service • Assign URL's to Benefit Plan Types** will lead you to the screen shown in Figure 5.14.

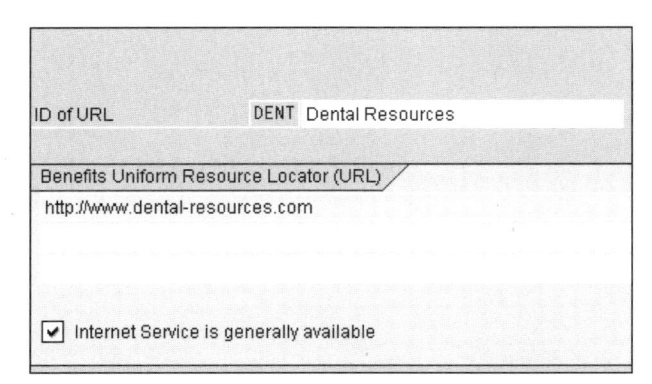

Figure 5.14 Assign URL to Plan Type

Another important benefit area to discuss is Payroll.

5.6 SAP Benefits in an Outsourced Payroll Environment

Today, many companies choose to use an outsourced payroll environment. The Benefits module in these cases needs to interface with the outsourced payroll environment. Such a scenario will look as follows:

- Benefits enrollment carried out in SAP
- Benefits infotypes are maintained in SAP
- Benefit infotypes have the employee (EE) and employer (ER) portions of the costs
- Outsourced payroll carries out the calcuations and actual deductions

Since our focus is on configuration and technical details, what is it that we need?

1. An export of employee data to the external payroll system. SAP has delivered an **Interface Toolbox** that you can access from the application menu **Payroll USA • Tools • Outsourcing Interface Toolbox • Data Export • Export.** Figure 5.15 shows the interface format usage in the interface toolbox. You can use the delivered formats or alternatively create new formats for the data transfer.

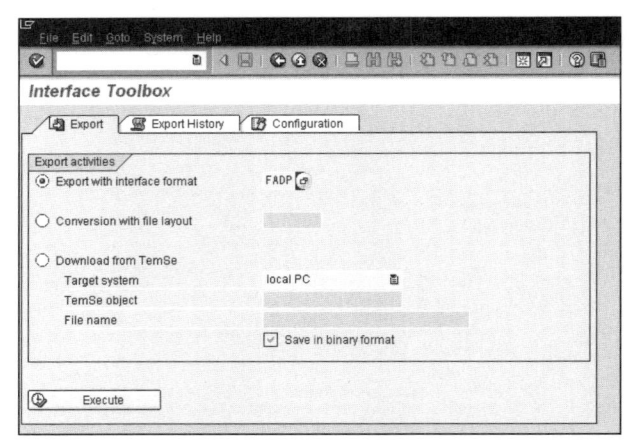

Figure 5.15 Using a Format in the Interface Toolbox

2. When an outsourced payroll environment runs the payroll, actual deductions are taken in the payroll system. Using the application menu path **Payroll USA • Tools • Outsourcing Interface Toolbox • Import • Payroll Import,** the results can be brought back into SAP. Some implementations choose not to bring the results back and keep it in the external payroll system.

3. All the downstream vendor interfaces need to be either carried out from the outsourced vendor payroll, or if the payroll results are brought back to SAP, then they will follow the normal path as we discussed in Section 5.3 earlier.

4. The financials and accounts payable postings need to follow the same philosophy — either directly from the payroll system or from SAP, if the results are brought back.

5.7 Benefits Schemas

The topic of benefits configuration would not be complete unless we visited the Benefits Schemas. In the US Payroll Schema U000, you will find two sub-schemas **UBE1** and **UBE2** as shown in Figure 5.16 and 5.17.

You will notice that sub-schema **UBE1** processes health plans (infotype 0167), insurance plans (infotype 0168), and miscellaneous plans (infotype 0377). While sub-schema **UBE2** processes savings plans (infotype 0169) and flexible spending accounts (infotype 0170). You will notice that infotype 0377 has a second call again in sub-schema **UBE2**. This is due to the fact that miscellaneous plans can be either used similar to Health, Insurance, or Savings plans, and therefore, it is processed in both the sub-schemas.

Edit Schema: UBE1						
Cmmnd						Stack
Line	Func.	Par1	Par2	Par3	Par4	D Text
000010	BLOCK	BEG				Process Benefits
000020	BENPR					Prepare Benefits Processing
000030	BENUS					prepare US Benefits Processing
000040	P0167	BEG				Process Health Plans
000050	P0168	BEG				Process Insurance Plans
000060	UGTLI					Process Group Term Life Insurance
000070	P0377	BEG	1			Process Miscellan. Pl. (1st call)
000080	P0236	BEG	1			Process Credit Plans (1st call)
000090	BLOCK	END				Process Benefits

Figure 5.16 Schema UBE1

Edit Schema: UBE2						
Cmmnd						Stack
Line	Func.	Par1	Par2	Par3	Par4	D Text
000010	BLOCK	BEG				Process Benefits (2nd part)
000020	BENCM					Process compensations
000030	P0170	CHK				Process Spending Accounts
000040	P0169	BEG				Process Savings Plans
000050	P0377	BEG	2			Process Miscellaneous Plans(2nd call)
000060	P0379	BEG				Process Stock Purchase Plans
000070	P0236	BEG	2			Process Credit Plans (2nd call)
000080	BLOCK	END				Process Benefits (2nd part)

Figure 5.17 Schema UBE2

In case, you decide to use custom rules in payroll related to benefits, then they need to be used in these, or after these, sub-schemas when benefits infotypes are read and processed.

5.8 Summary

As we have seen in this chapter, the Benefits module is a little more technology-heavy than the other SAP HR modules, such as PA, OM, and Payroll. The Benefits module also requires the most interfaces compared to other SAP HR modules, and it is normally at the top of the list for ESS applications. Many companies use ESS for benefits due to immediate Return on Investment (ROI). Hopefully, this chapter has given you a solid introduction to the different technology elements of the Benefits module. Unfortunately we could not cover them in more detail, because each of the elements could really be the subject of its own book!

With this chapter we conclude the book. We hope that the details provided about the typical benefits plan configuration, and the technical tools that are useful during implementation of the SAP Benefits module, will guide you successfully through your own benefits configuration. You can send your feedback to *saphrwriter@yahoo.com*. Best wished on your SAP US Benefits journey.

A   Life Plan Configuration Sheet

Configuration Required	Explanation
Insurance Plans	
Plan Basics	
Plan Type	Life
Plan Name	Name
Provider	Vendor
Status of plan	Open, Locked
Automatic Plan	Yes/No
Default Plan	Yes/No
Program Groupings	
Eligible personnel area	To determine program groupings
Eligible personnel sub-area	To determine program groupings
Eligible employee group	To determine program groupings
Eligible employee sub-group	To determine program groupings
Full Time/Part Time	Eligibility
Number of hours in work schedule	20 hours and less condition
Coverage	
1X Salary	One time salary
2X Salary	Two time salary
3X Salary	Three times salary
4X Salary	Four times salary
5X Salary	Five times salary

Configuration Required	Explanation
Cost Critera	
Age	Define the age based rules
Salary	Define the salary based rules
Length of Service	Define the length of service based rule
Coverage Amount	Coverage amount for cost
Smoker/Non Smoker	Indicator
EE Cost	Employee cost
ER Cost	Employer cost
Provider Cost	Provider cost
Imputed Income indicator	Imputed income Yes/No
Evidence of Insurability (EOI)	EOI required indicator
Eligibility Rules	
Employee eligibility	Define the employee eligibility rule
Dependent eligibility	Define dependent eligibility rule
Termination Rules	
Employee	Define employee termination rule. Example — Termination on last day of the month
Dependent	Define dependent termination rule

B Model Wage Types for Benefits

Delivered Model Wage Type	Long Text
Employee Portion	
BA10	Std Medical EE after-tax
BA11	Medical 2 EE after-tax
BA12	Vision EE after-tax
BA13	Group Ins EE after-tax
BA14	Medical HMO EE after-tax
BA15	Indemn 90/10 EE after-tax
BA16	Indemn 80/20 EE after-tax
BA17	Medical PPO EE after-tax
BA18	Retiree Med EE after-tax
BA19	Medical DP EE after-tax
BA20	Basic Life EE after-tax
BA21	LTD EE after-tax
BA22	Dep Life EE after-tax
BA23	Opt Life EE after-tax
BA24	AD&D EE after-tax
BA25	Life 5 EE after-tax
BA26	STD EE after-tax
BA27	Travel EE after-tax
BA30	Savings EE after-tax
BA31	401k EE after-tax
BA32	Cash Bal EE after-tax
BA33	Thrift EE after-tax
BA34	Savings 3 EE after-tax
BA35	Savings 4 EE after-tax
BA36	Pension EE post-tax
BA50	Car EE after-tax
BA51	Fitness EE after-tax
BA52	Legal Ins EE after-tax
BA53	Charity EE after-tax
BA54	Vacation Buy EE after-tax
BA60	EAP EE after-tax
BA61	Health Club EE after-tax
BA62	Pension EE after-tax
BA63	Defer Comp-S EE after-tax
BA64	Defer Comp-B EE after-tax
BA65	Vac Buy EE after-tax
BA70	Stock Purch EE after-tax
BA71	Alt Stock EE after-tax
BC31	EE age catch-up contrib
BC35	Pension1 Compensation
BC36	Pension2 Compensation
BC37	Grandf.Pens. Compensation
BC40	(CL) Spending Acct. clm.
BE10	Std Medical EE pre-tax
BE11	Dental EE pre-tax
BE12	Vision EE pre-tax
BE13	Group Ins EE pre-tax
BE14	Medical HMO EE pre-tax
BE15	Indemnity90/10 EE pre-tax
BE16	Indemnity80/20 EE pre-tax
BE17	Medical PPO EE pre-tax
BE18	Retiree Med EE pre-tax
BE19	Medical DP EE pre-tax
BE20	Basic Life EE pre-tax
BE21	LTD EE pre-tax

A Model Wage Types for Benefits

Delivered Model Wage Type	Long Text
BE22	Dep Life EE pre-tax
BE23	Opt Life EE pre-tax
BE24	AD&D EE pre-tax
BE25	Life 5 EE pre-tax
BE26	STD EE pre-tax
BE27	Travel EE pre-tax
BE28	Supp. Life Insurance
BE30	Savings EE Pre-tax
BE31	401k EE pre-tax
BE32	403b EE pre-tax
BE33	Thrift EE pre-tax
BE34	457 EE pre-tax
BE35	Savings 4 EE pre-tax
BE36	Pension EE pre-tax
BE3A	401K deduction
BE3P	401K deduction
BE40	Health Care EE pre-tax
BE41	Dep Care EE pre-tax
BE50	Car EE pre-tax
BE51	Fitness EE pre-tax
BE52	Legal Ins EE pre-tax
BE53	Charity EE pre-tax
BE54	Vacation Buy EE pre-tax
BE60	EAP EE pre-tax
BE61	Health Club EE pre-tax
BE62	Pension EE pre-tax
BE63	Defer Comp-S EE pre-tax
BE64	Defer Comp-B EE pre-tax
BE65	Vac Buy EE pre-tax
BE70	Stock Purch EE pre-tax
BE80	EE age catch-up contrib
BM19	Med DP Imputed Income
Provider Costs	
BP10	Std Medical Provider

Delivered Model Wage Type	Long Text
BP11	Dental Provider
BP12	Vision Provider
BP13	Group Ins Provider
BP14	Medical HMO Provider
BP15	Indemnity 90/10 Provider
BP16	Indemnity 80/20 Provider
BP17	Medical PPO Provider
BP18	Retiree Med Provider
BP19	Medical DP Provider
BP20	Basic Life Provider
BP21	LTD Provider
BP22	Dep Life Provider
BP23	Opt Life Provider
BP24	AD&D Provider
BP25	Life 5 Provider
BP26	STD Provider
BP27	Travel Provider
BP31	401k Provider
BP32	Cash Bal Provider
BP33	Thrift Provider
BP34	Savings 3 Provider
BP35	Savings 4 Provider
BP50	Car Provider
BP51	Fitness Provider
BP52	Legal Ins Provider
BP60	EAP Provider
BP61	Health Club Provider
BP62	Pension Provider
BP63	Defer Comp-S Provider
BP64	Defer Comp-B Provider
BP65	Vac Buy Provider
Employer Costs/Portion	
BR10	Std Medical Employer
BR11	Dental Employer

A Model Wage Types for Benefits

Delivered Model Wage Type	Long Text
BR12	Vision Employer
BR13	Group Ins Employer
BR14	Medical HMO Employer
BR15	Indemnity 90/10 Employer
BR16	Indemnity 80/20 Employer
BR17	Medical PPO Employer
BR18	Retiree Med Employer
BR19	Medical DP Employer
BR20	Basic Life Employer
BR21	LTD Employer
BR22	Dep Life Employer
BR23	Opt Life Employer
BR24	AD&D Employer
BR25	Life 5 Employer
BR26	STD Employer
BR27	Travel Employer
BR28	Supp. Life Insurance
BR30	Savings Employer
BR31	401k Employer
BR32	403b Employer
BR33	Thrift Employer
BR34	457 Employer
BR35	Savings 4 Employer
BR36	Pension Employer contr.
BR40	Health Care Employer
BR41	Dependent care Employer
BR50	Flex Credit 1 Employer
BR51	Flex Credit 2 Employer
BR52	Legal Ins Employer
BR53	Charity Employer
BR54	Vacation Buy Employer
BR60	EAP Employer
BR61	Health Club Employer
BR62	Pension Employer
BR63	Defer Comp-S Employer
BR64	Defer Comp-B Employer
BR65	Vac Buy Employer
BR70	Stock Purch Employer
BR71	Alt Stock Employer
BSAL	Benefit-based salary

C Typical Benefits Terminology Questions

Listed below are the sample questions that many SAP configurators have related to definitions for various terminologies used in benefits. These answers are only indicative representation, so please verify the local laws and regulations for the accurate answers. The questions and answers are in no particular order or priority.

1. What is a 401k pre-tax limit?
For years 2007 and 2008, a pre-tax limit of $15,500 is mandated by the IRS. Therefore, an employee who elects to participate in 401k or related retirement plans, can contribute a pre-tax/before-tax maximum of $15,500 to the 401k account.

2. Can you do post-tax/after-tax contributions to 401k?
That will depend upon your plan offerings and some 401k plans do offer a post tax contribution.

3. What is a catch-up contribution?
Those participants who are or will turn 50 years of age are eligible to contribute $5000 to their 401k accounts. However, there is a condition that needs to be met. The participant's regular plan contribution must meet one of the following conditions:
- Annual limit
- Plan's annual limit (if any)
- Annual ADP limit for HCE employees (please refer to the ADP and HCE definitions in this Appendix)

4. What is ADP?
The Actual Deferral Percentage (ADP) test is meant for HCE employees and for the successful test, the elective contributions for 401k plan, must satisfy one of the conditions listed here:

- Basic Limit: The ADP for a group of HCE employees cannot be more than 125 % for the group of eligible non-HCE employees
- Alternative Limit: The ADP for a group of eligible HCE's cannot be more than 2 % greater than the ADP of a group of non-HCE eligible employees, and the ADP for a group of eligible HCE's cannot be more than 2 times the ADP for the group of eligible non-HCE's.

5. What is HCE?
A Highly Compensated Employee (HCE) is the one who:
- Owns more than 5 % interest in the business during any time of the year in the previous year
- Received compensation of more than $100,000 in the preceding year (2007 limits)
- You can also choose top 20 % employees by compensation rank as HCE cases.

6. What is a Pre-tax/Before tax deduction?
The pre-tax or before-tax deductions are taken out of the employee's gross salaray before the taxes are calculated. As a result the base for tax calculation is reduced and an employee gets the advantage. The Health and Savings plans deductions are normally pre-tax with applicable limits as prescribed by the IRS.

7. What is a Post-tax/After tax deduction?
The post-tax or after-tax deductions are the deductions taken out of the employee's salary after the taxes are calculated. The deductions such as union dues or united way contributions are typically post-tax in nature.

8. What are the different types of salary deferral plans?
The different types of savings/salary deferral plans are as follows:

A Typical Benefits Terminology Questions

- 401(k) Plans: These are generally sponsored by private as well as public sector companies
- 403(b) Plans: These are typically sponsored by non-profit organizations for their employees
- 457(b): These are for Government employees
- SIMPLE: For small businesses

9. What is COBRA?
COBRA stands for Consolidated Omnibus Budget Reconciliation Act (COBRA). Please refer to the COBRA details in Chapter 1 of this book.

10. How do you define a Dependent?
The IRS definition for dependents fall into two categories: Qualifying Child and Qualifying Relative.

For both qualifying child and qualifying relatives, there are five tests that are applied, including relationship, gross income, support, joint filing and residency. Please refer to the IRS web site for additional details.

11. How do you define a Beneficiary and is the spouse a primary beneficiary for the 401k unless the right is waved?
Upon death of the participant, a person or persons receive the benefits of the plan, for example, the 401k plan or retirement plan. You can normally name primary and secondary beneficiaries. The federal law mandates that the surviving spouse is the primary beneficiary of a 401k plan, unless the spouse signs a timely effective written waiver.

12. What is HIPAA?
The US Department of Health and Human Services (HHS) issued a privacy rule under the Health Insurance Portability and Accountability Act. This act provides privacy rule standards related to an individual's health information and how it is used and disclosed by the organizations. You will find more information on the HHS web site. (*www.hhs.gov*).

13. What is a HIPAA 834?
It is a format that established the data contents for benefits enrollment and maintenance transactions for use within the context of the Electronic Data Interchange (EDI) environment. For example, data going from your system to the provider system after new hire enrollment.

14. What is EOI?
Typically to get high levels of life insurance you need to demonstrate good health by providing "Evidence of Insurability" (EOI). For basic employee life insurance, EOI is normally not required, but for employee supplemental and dependent life insurances, the EOI conditions are applicable.

15. How do you define Base Salary for Benefits?
The salary that is used for the 401k percentage contribution calculation is the base salary. It is generally the same as gross salary.

16. What is a 401k contribution %?
This is the percent of their salary that an employee decides to contribute pre-tax to the 401k plan. The base salary then is used to calculate the amount and the amount is used to distribute into the funds selected by the employee. The employer contribution portion depends upon company policies and is directly related to the employee contribution percent.

17. What is the meaning of Imputed Income?
It is the term the IRS applies to the value of benefits or service that should be considered income for the purpose of federal taxes. For example, an employer provided life insurance policy more than $50,000.

18. What is a Dependent Age Out?
Typically dependent children include those who are under 19 years of age and for whom the employee provides primary support and also claims in the tax filing as dependents. Until the age of 24, the child can be covered as dependent, if the child is enrolled in an accredited college program. The dependent age-out is the term used when the dependent child reaches the 19th or 24th birthday as explained above. Therefore, coverage of the dependent child will end accordingly.

19. Are there special provisions for Disabled Dependents?
An over-age dependent child beyond the 19/24 years limit as explained above and who is termed disabled as per the physician's proof can continue to receive the coverage.

20. What is the meaning of Co-requisite plan?

A co-requisite plan is where two plans have to co-exist. The employee will have to enroll in both plans together.

21. What is the meaning of Pre-requisite plan?

If two plans have a pre-requisite relationship then the employee needs to be enrolled in the pre-requisite plan at least a day before enrolling in the second plan.

22. What is health benefits waiver?

An employee may choose to waive the health plan benefits since the employee may be covered under the spouse's health plan. Normally, the employee will have to sign a waiver form.

23. What is a combined contribution limit?

If an employee is enrolled in more than one type of 401k plan, the limits are still decided by the combined or total contribution across plans.

24. What is a qualified plan?

A qualified plan is the one established by an employer to provide retirement benefits to the employees.

25. What is an ERISA?

The Employee Retirement Income Security Act (ERISA) protects the retirement assets. The act ensures that the fiduciaries do not misuse the assets.

Index

A

Action reason 21
Action type 21
Adjustment permissions 52
Adjustment reason 22, 23, 24, 46, 48
   groupings 22
ADP 69
after-tax 69
Age group 28, 31
Annual pre-tax limit 36
Authorization 14

B

Base unit 34
Beneficiary 70
Benefit infotypes 47, 50
Benefit programs 18
Benefit provider 6, 15, 16, 57
Benefit providers 57
Benefits adjustment reasons 45
Benefits administration 6
Benefits Administrator 8
Benefits area 13, 14, 23, 32
Benefits enrollment 45
Benefits Monitor 48
Benefits Termination 49
Bonus contributions 36

C

Catch-up contribution 37
Changes to Benefits 8
Claim types 39
Claims 39
COBRA 6, 9, 41, 50, 55
   elections 50
   enrollment 50
   events 50
   participation monitor 50
Combined annual limits 35

Configuration Consistency Check 52
Confirmation letters 8
Constant table 36
Continuation of coverage 42
Contribution amounts 29
Contribution limits 35
Contribution rule 36
Contribution variant 35, 37, 40
Co-requisite 71
Cost factor 34
Cost grouping 28, 31
Cost rule 32, 40
Cost rules 31, 34, 41
Cost variant 31, 32, 34, 40, 41
Coverage amount 34
Coverage groupings 29
Coverage options 31
Coverage rule 33
Coverage variant 33, 34, 40

D

Data conversion 58
Date specifications 20
Define cost variants 31
Dependent 70
Dependent Age Out 70
Dependent care 10, 38
Dependent Children 10
dependent coverage 32
Dependent coverage options 31
Dependent eligibility 20
Dependent eligibility rule 20
Dependent eligibility variant 20
Disable Dependents 70
Dynamic eligibility 20

E

EBSA 6
Election changes 49

Eligibility 27
Eligibility criteria 8
Eligibility groupings 18
Eligibility rule 18, 19, 51, 57
Eligibility variants 19
Employee contribution 30
Employee contribution grouping 29
Employee contribution rules 36
Employee contribution variants 35, 37
Employee cost 27
Employee criteria groups 27
Employee groupings 27
Employee life cycle 6
Employee life event 48
Employee Self Service (ESS) 8, 58, 59
Employer contribution grouping 30
Employer contribution variant 37
Employer cost 27
Enrollment 7, 24, 58
Enrollment confirmation 55
Enrollment monitor 24, 45, 46
Entitlement for COBRA 9
EOI 70
ERISA 71

F

Feature 29
FICA 34
First and second program groupings 15, 16
First program grouping 16, 29
Flexible administration 21
Flexible spending accounts 38, 58
Flexible Spending Plans 8
Forms 55
FSA 38
Function module 56

Index

G
Group term life insurance 32

H
HCE 69
Health Care 10, 38
Health plan 8, 30, 32
HIPAA 6, 70
Homepage Framework 59
HR payee 15, 27
HR structures 13, 15, 17, 18, 19, 20, 28, 29

I
IDoc 57
Imputed income 33, 34
Infotype 0167 32
Infotype 0169 38
Infotype 0171 38
Infotype 0267 36
Infotypes 8
Insurance Plans 8, 32
Interfaces 57
Investment groups 38
Investments 37

L
Life event date 48
Life events 5, 8, 22, 45, 48
Long-term disability 57

M
Miscellaneous plan attributes 40
Miscellaneous plans 40, 41

N
New hire 6, 7, 46
New hire event 46

O
Open enrollment 45, 49
Open enrollment period 8
Options 30, 32
Outbound 57

P
Parameter group 27, 28, 31, 33, 36
Parameter groupings 43
Personnel action 8, 13, 42, 49
Plan attributes 32, 34, 41
Plan categories 16
Plan Cost Summary 51
Plan costs 51
Plan general data 30, 33, 35, 40
Plan Overview 51
Plan status 16, 30
Plan type 16, 30
Post-tax limits 36
Pre-requisite 71
Pre-tax deduction 30
Pre-tax limits 35, 36, 69
Previous year claims 38
Processing parameters 42
Provider cost 27

Q
Qualified Beneficiaries 10
Qualified COBRA Events 10
Qualified events 41
Qualified expenses 38
Qualified plan 71
Qualifying COBRA event 42
Qualifying events 42

S
Salary deferral plans 69
Salary group 28, 31
SAPscript 55
Savings plan attributes 37
Savings Plans 8, 35
Second program grouping 17
Seniority groups 28

T
Telephone-based systems 8
Termination 6, 9, 21
Termination groupings 21
Termination monitor 24, 49
Termination rules 18, 22, 51
Termination variant 22

U
User exits 56

V
Vesting rule 37, 41

W
Work Events 8

ISBN 978-1-59229-164-9
1st edition 2008
© 2008 by Galileo Press GmbH
SAP PRESS is an imprint of Galileo Press,
Boston (MA), USA
Bonn, Germany

Editor Jennifer Niles
Copy Editor John Parker, UCG, Inc., Boston, MA
Cover Design Katrin Müller
Production Steffi Ehrentraut
Printed in Germany

All rights reserved. Neither this publication nor any part of it may be copied or reproduced in any form or by any means or translated into another language, without the prior consent of Galileo Press, Rheinwerkallee 4, 53227 Bonn, Germany.

Galileo Press makes no warranties or representations with respect to the content hereof and specifically disclaims any implied warranties of merchantability or fitness for any particular purpose. Galileo Press assumes no reponsibility for any errors that may appear in this publication.

All of the screenshots and graphics reproduced in this book are subject to copyright © SAP AG, Dietmar-Hopp-Allee 16, 69190 Walldorf, Germany.

SAP, the SAP-Logo, mySAP, SAP NetWeaver, mySAP Business Suite, mySAP.com, SAP R/3, SAP R/2, SAP B2B, SAPtronic, SAPscript, SAP BW, SAP CRM, SAP EarlyWatch, SAP ArchiveLink, SAP GUI, SAP Business Workflow, SAP Business Engineer, SAP Business Navigator, SAP Business Framework, SAP Business Information Warehouse, SAP inter-enterprise solutions, SAP APO, AcceleratedSAP, InterSAP, SAPoffice, SAPfind, SAPfile, SAPtime, SAPmail, SAPaccess, SAP-EDI, R/3 Retail, Accelerated HR, Accelerated HiTech, Accelerated Consumer Products, ABAP, ABAP/4, ALE/ WEB, BAPI, Business Framework, BW Explorer, Enjoy-SAP, mySAP.com e-business platform, mySAP Enterprise Portals, RIVA, SAPPHIRE, TeamSAP, Webflow and SAP PRESS are registered or unregistered trademarks of SAP AG, Walldorf.

All other products mentioned in this book are registered or unregistered trademarks of their respective companies.